Comfort FOOD

p

This is a Parragon Book
First Published in 2005

Parragon
Queen Street House
4 Queen Street
Bath BA1 1HE
United Kingdom

Design: Shelley Doyle - 20 Twenty Design

ISBN: 1-40546-060-1

Printed in China

NOTE

This book uses metric and imperial measurements. Follow the same units of measurement throughout; do not mix metric and imperial. All spoon measurements are level: teaspoons are assumed to be 5 ml and tablespoons are assumed to be 15 ml. Unless otherwise stated, milk is assumed to be full fat, eggs and individual vegetables such as potatoes are medium, and pepper is freshly ground black pepper.

The times given for each recipe are an approximate guide only because the preparation times may differ according to the techniques used by different people and the cooking times may vary as a result of the type of oven and other equipment used.

Recipes using raw or very lightly cooked eggs should be avoided by infants, the elderly, pregnant women, convalescents and anyone suffering from an illness. Pregnant and breast-feeding women are advised to avoid eating peanuts and peanut products.

Contents

Contents

Introduction p4

Sweet Indulgence p6

Soothing Savoury p48

Quick Fixes p90

Index p128

Introduction

Introduction

There is nothing in the world quite like a bowl full of something hearty or a slice of something sweet just to make you feel the world is a better place. When life is grey and cold, savour a little domestic warmth with simple food that lifts the spirits and nourishes body and soul.

The dishes we celebrate as our favourite 'comfort foods' are the treats that are often highly evocative of a time or place that is familiar and positive. Whether you are a sweet treats supporter, or whether you opt for soothing savoury dishes, these pages contain the perfect blues-busters.

The warm and welcoming aroma of the kitchen is often the starting place for many traditional comfort foods. These delicious filling dishes offer a feeling of calm and contentment that is frequently associated with childhood. Food has an extremely powerful effect on the memory and many people remember habitual family meals, home-cooked favourites, school dinners and enduring classic dishes. This type of cooking provides therapy not only in the eating but also in the preparation, as methodical slicing, stirring and beating slows the mind and offers a physical outlet for today's hectic lifestyle. The iconic image of pure savoury comfort food is a life-saving, thick, warm meal for the times when the rain is battering on the window pane.

But what about a delectable bowl of soft, rich ice cream when you are curled up in front of the television? Or a plate of pancakes dripping in maple sauce? Aahh yes, the joy of sweet comfort foods. A sugary pick-me-up and a sense that 'we really shouldn't' will make sweet treats all the more inviting. Warm muffins and scones are fantastic with a mug of tea or coffee and can chase away those blues. Recent research suggests that women are more likely to reach for sweet comfort foods as they often require less labour intensive preparation and offer instant gratification. Again, however, the lure of a warm kitchen calls with many traditional puddings and cakes provoking heart-warming memories of the family hearth. Time-honoured cooking conventions have a lot to be said for them, as home-baked cakes will keep you feeling fuller and more satisfied than store-bought confectionary.

Comfort food is essentially concerned with the simple pleasures in life. The recipes in this book are sometimes humble, occasionally solid or sticky but always friendly and reassuring. Good quality wholesome ingredients are a must when preparing them, and sharing this delicious fare with friends or family will make you feel even better!

Sweet Indulgence

Sweet Indulgence

There is something immediately comforting about a sweet treat, giving you a ray of sunshine to revive your spirits. A huge bowl of delectable Raspberry Ripple Ice Cream is the perfect accompaniment to your favourite film and a gorgeous Chocolate Fudge Cake will put a smile on your face no matter what the season or weather.

Apple & Plum Crumble

Apple & Plum Crumble

SERVES 4

4 apples, peeled, cored and diced

5 plums, halved, stoned and quartered

4 tbsp fresh apple juice

25 g/1 oz soft light brown sugar

FOR THE TOPPING

115 g/4 oz plain flour

75 g/2¾ oz margarine, diced

25 g/1 oz buckwheat flakes

25 g/1 oz rice flakes

25 g/1 oz sunflower seeds

50 g/1¾ oz soft light brown sugar

¼ tsp ground cinnamon

1. Preheat the oven to 180°C/350°F/Gas Mark 4. Mix the apples, plums, apple juice and sugar together in a 23-cm/9-inch round pie dish.

2. To make the topping, sift the flour into a mixing bowl and rub in the margarine with your fingertips until it resembles coarse breadcrumbs. Stir in the buckwheat and rice flakes, sunflower seeds, sugar and cinnamon, then spoon the topping over the fruit in the dish.

3. Bake the crumble in the preheated oven for 30–35 minutes, or until the topping is lightly browned and crisp.

Rich Vanilla Ice Cream

Rich Vanilla Ice Cream

SERVES 4 – 6

300 ml/10 fl oz single cream and

300 ml/10 fl oz double cream or

600 ml/1 pint whipping cream

1 vanilla pod

4 large egg yolks

115 g/4 oz caster sugar

1. Pour the single and double cream or whipping cream into a large heavy-based saucepan. Split open the vanilla pod and scrape out the seeds into the cream, then add the whole vanilla pod too. Bring almost to the boil, then remove from the heat and leave to infuse for 30 minutes.

2. Put the egg yolks and sugar in a large bowl and whisk together until pale and the mixture leaves a trail when the whisk is lifted. Remove the vanilla pod from the cream, then slowly add the cream to the egg mixture, stirring all the time with a wooden spoon. Strain the mixture into the rinsed-out saucepan or a double boiler and cook over a low heat for 10–15 minutes, stirring all the time, until the mixture thickens enough to coat the back of the spoon. Do not allow the mixture to boil or it will curdle. Remove the custard from the heat and leave to cool for at least 1 hour, stirring from time to time to prevent a skin from forming.

3. If using an ice cream machine, churn the cold custard in the machine following the manufacturer's instructions. Alternatively, freeze the custard in a freezerproof container, uncovered, for 1–2 hours, or until it begins to set around the edges. Turn the custard into a bowl and stir with a fork or beat in a food processor until smooth. Return to the freezer and freeze for a further 2–3 hours, or until firm or required. Cover the container with a lid for storing.

Profiteroles

SERVES 4

CHOUX PASTRY

5 tbsp butter, plus extra for greasing

200 ml/7 fl oz water

100 g/3½ oz plain flour

3 eggs, beaten

CREAM FILLING

300 ml/10 fl oz double cream

3 tbsp caster sugar

1 tsp vanilla essence

CHOCOLATE & BRANDY SAUCE

125 g/4½ oz plain chocolate, broken into small pieces

2½ tbsp butter

6 tbsp water

2 tbsp brandy

1. Preheat the oven to 200°C/400°F/Gas Mark 6. Grease a large baking sheet with butter. To make the pastry, put the water and butter into a saucepan and bring to the boil. Meanwhile, sift the flour into a bowl. Remove the pan from the heat and beat in the flour until smooth. Cool for 5 minutes. Beat in enough of the eggs to give the mixture a soft, dropping consistency. Transfer to a piping bag fitted with a 1-cm/½-inch plain nozzle. Pipe small balls onto the baking sheet. Bake for 25 minutes. Remove from the oven. Pierce each ball with a skewer to let steam escape.

2. To make the filling, whip together the cream, sugar and vanilla essence. Cut the pastry balls almost in half, then fill with cream.

3. To make the sauce, gently melt the chocolate and butter with the water together in a small saucepan, stirring, until smooth. Stir in the brandy. Pile the profiteroles into individual serving dishes or into a pyramid on a raised cake stand. Pour over the sauce and serve.

Chelsea Buns

MAKES 9

25 g/1 oz butter, plus extra for greasing

225 g/8 oz strong white bread flour, plus extra for dusting

$^1/_2$ tsp salt

2 tsp easy-blend dried yeast

1 tsp golden caster sugar

125 ml/4 fl oz tepid milk

1 egg, beaten

vegetable oil, for brushing

85 g/3 oz icing sugar, to glaze

FILLING

55 g/2 oz light muscovado sugar

115 g/4 oz luxury mixed dried fruits

1 tsp ground mixed spice

55 g/2 oz butter, softened

1. Grease an 18-cm/7-inch square cake tin. Sift the flour and salt into a warmed bowl, stir in the yeast and sugar and rub in the butter. Make a well in the centre. In a separate bowl, mix the milk and egg and pour into the dry ingredients. Beat to make a soft dough. Turn out onto a floured work surface and knead for 5–10 minutes, or until smooth. Brush a clean bowl with oil, place the dough in the bowl, cover with clingfilm and leave in a warm place for 1 hour, or until doubled in size.

2. Turn the dough out onto a floured surface and knead lightly for 1 minute. Roll out into a 30 x 23-cm/12 x 9-inch rectangle.

3. To make the filling, place the muscovado sugar, fruit and spice in a bowl and mix. Spread the dough with the softened butter and sprinkle the fruit mixture on top. Roll up from a long side, then cut into 9 pieces. Place in the prepared tin, cut-side up. Cover with oiled clingfilm and leave in a warm place for 45 minutes, or until well risen.

4. Preheat the oven to 190°C/375°F/Gas Mark 5. Bake the buns in the oven for 30 minutes, or until golden. Leave to cool in the tin for 10 minutes, then transfer, in one piece, to a wire rack to cool. Sift the icing sugar into a bowl and stir in enough water to make a thin glaze. Brush over the buns and leave to set. Pull the buns apart to serve.

Raspberry Ripple Ice Cream

Raspberry Ripple Ice Cream

SERVES 6

85 g/3 oz fresh or frozen raspberries,

thawed if frozen, plus extra to serve

2 tbsp water

2 eggs

1 tbsp caster sugar

300 ml/10 fl oz milk, warmed

1 tsp vanilla extract

300 ml/10 fl oz double cream

1. Turn the freezer to rapid. Put the raspberries into a saucepan with the water and bring to the boil, then reduce the heat and simmer gently for 5 minutes. Remove from the heat and leave to cool for 30 minutes.

2. Transfer to a food processor or blender and process to a purée, then rub through a nylon sieve to remove the pips. Reserve.

3. Beat the eggs in a bowl. Stir the sugar into the warmed milk, then slowly pour onto the eggs, beating constantly. Strain into a clean saucepan and cook over a low heat, stirring constantly, for 8–10 minutes, or until the custard thickens and coats the back of a wooden spoon. Add the vanilla extract, remove from the heat and leave to cool.

4. Half-whip the cream in a large bowl, then slowly stir in the cooled custard. Pour into a freezerproof container and freeze for 1½ hours, or until beginning to set around the outside. Remove from the freezer and stir the mixture, breaking up any ice crystals.

5. Return the mixture to the freezer and freeze for a further hour, then remove from the freezer and gently stir in the raspberry purée to give a rippled effect. Return to the freezer for a further hour or until frozen. Serve in scoops with extra fresh raspberries.

Chocolate Chip Muffins

Chocolate Chip Muffins

MAKES 12

100 g/3½ oz butter, softened

125 g/4½ oz caster sugar

100 g/3½ oz dark muscovado sugar

2 eggs

150 ml/5 fl oz soured cream

5 tbsp milk

250 g/9 oz plain flour

1 tsp bicarbonate of soda

2 tbsp unsweetened cocoa powder

190 g/6½ oz dark chocolate chips

1. Preheat the oven to 190°C/375°F/Gas Mark 5. Line a 12-ring muffin tin with paper cases.
2. Put the butter, caster sugar and dark muscovado sugar into a bowl and beat well. Beat in the eggs, cream and milk until thoroughly mixed. Sift the flour, bicarbonate of soda and cocoa powder into a separate bowl and stir into the mixture. Add the chocolate chips and mix well. Spoon the mixture into the paper cases. Bake in the oven for 25–30 minutes.
3. Remove from the oven and leave to cool for 10 minutes. Turn out onto a wire rack and leave to cool completely. Store in an airtight container until required.

Fine Chocolate Tart

SERVES 6

PASTRY

125 g/4½ oz plain flour

2 tsp cocoa powder

2 tsp icing sugar

pinch of salt

50 g/1¾ oz cold butter, cut into pieces

1 egg yolk

ice-cold water

GANACHE FILLING

200 g/7 oz plain chocolate with 70% cocoa solids

25 g/1 oz unsalted butter, softened

240 ml/8 fl oz double cream

1 tsp dark rum (optional)

1 Lightly butter a 22-cm/9-inch loose-bottomed fluted tart tin. Sift the flour, cocoa powder, icing sugar and salt into a food processor, add the butter and process until the mixture resembles fine breadcrumbs. Tip the mixture into a large bowl, add the egg yolk and add a little ice-cold water, just enough to bring the dough together. Turn out onto a surface dusted with more flour and cocoa powder and roll out the pastry 8 cm/3¼ inches larger than the tin. Carefully lift the pastry into the tin and press to fit. Roll the rolling pin over the tin to neaten the edges and trim the excess pastry. Fit a piece of baking paper into the tart case, fill with baking beans and chill in the refrigerator for 30 minutes. Meanwhile, preheat the oven to 190°C/375°F/Gas Mark 5.

2 Remove the pastry case from the refrigerator and bake the pastry for 15 minutes in the preheated oven then remove the beans and paper and bake for a further 5 minutes.

3 To make the ganache filling, chop the chocolate and put in a bowl with the softened butter. Bring the cream to the boil then pour onto the chocolate, stirring well, add the rum (if using) and continue stirring to make sure the chocolate is melted completely. Pour into the pastry case and chill for 3 hours.

Latticed Cherry Pie

Latticed Cherry Pie

SERVES 8

PASTRY

140 g/5 oz plain flour, plus extra for dusting

1/4 tsp baking powder

3/4 tsp mixed spice

1/2 tsp salt

200 g/7 oz caster sugar

6 tbsp cold unsalted butter, diced,

plus extra for greasing

water, for sealing

1 beaten egg, plus extra for glazing

FILLING

900 g/2 lb stoned fresh cherries, or canned

cherries, drained

1/2 tsp almond extract

2 tsp cherry brandy

2 tbsp cornflour

2 tbsp water

freshly whipped cream or ice cream, to serve

1 To make the pastry, sift the flour with the baking powder into a large bowl. Stir in 1/2 tsp mixed spice, 1/2 tsp salt and 50 g/1 3/4 oz sugar. Using your fingertips, rub in 4 tablespoons of butter until the mixture resembles fine breadcrumbs, then make a well in the centre. Pour the beaten egg into the well. Mix with a wooden spoon, then shape the mixture into a dough. Cut the dough in half, and use your hands to roll each half into a ball. Wrap the dough and chill in the refrigerator for 30 minutes.

2 Preheat the oven to 220°C/425°F/Gas Mark 7. Grease a 23-cm/9-inch round pie dish with butter. Roll out the pastry into 2 rounds, each 30 cm/12 inches in diameter. Use one to line the pie dish. Trim the edge, leaving an overhang of 1 cm/1/2 inch.

3 To make the filling, put half of the cherries and the remaining sugar in a large saucepan. Bring to a simmer over a low heat, stirring, for 5 minutes, or until the sugar has melted. Stir in the almond extract, brandy and remaining mixed spice. In a separate bowl, mix the cornflour and water to form a paste. Remove the saucepan from the heat, stir in the cornflour paste, then return to the heat and stir constantly until the mixture boils and thickens. Leave to cool a little. Stir in the remaining cherries, pour into the pastry case, then dot with the remaining butter.

4 Cut the remaining pastry round into long strips 1 cm/1/2 inch wide. Lay 5 strips evenly across the top of the filling in the same direction, folding back every other strip. Now lay 6 strips crossways over the strips, folding back every other strip each time you add another crossways strip, to form a lattice. Trim off the ends and seal the edges with water. Use your fingers to crimp around the rim, then brush the top with beaten egg to glaze. Cover with kitchen foil, then bake for 30 minutes. Remove from the oven, discard the foil, then return the pie to the oven for a further 15 minutes, or until cooked and golden. Serve warm with freshly whipped cream or ice cream.

Mississippi Mud Cake

Mississippi Mud Cake

SERVES 16

250 g/9 oz butter, cut into pieces,

plus extra for greasing

150 g/5 1/2 oz plain chocolate

425 g/15 oz golden caster sugar

250 ml/9 fl oz hot water

3 tbsp coffee liqueur or brandy

250 g/9 oz plain flour

1 tsp baking powder

25 g/1 oz cocoa powder

2 eggs, beaten

fresh raspberries and chocolate curls, to serve

1. Preheat the oven to 160°C/325°F/Gas Mark 3, then grease and line a 20-cm/8-inch round cake tin. Break the chocolate into pieces, then place the butter, chocolate, sugar, hot water and coffee liqueur in a large, heavy-based saucepan over a low heat and stir until the chocolate melts.

2. Stir until smooth, transfer the mixture to a large bowl and leave to cool for 15 minutes. Sift in the flour, baking powder and cocoa and whisk in, then whisk in the eggs. Pour the mixture into the prepared cake tin.

3. Bake in the preheated oven for 1 1/2 hours, or until risen and firm to the touch. Leave to cool in the tin for 30 minutes, then turn out and peel off the lining paper. Transfer to a wire rack to cool completely. Decorate with fresh raspberries and chocolate curls and serve.

Manhattan Cheesecake

Manhattan Cheesecake

SERVES 8 – 10

sunflower oil, for brushing

85 g/3 oz butter

200 g/7 oz digestive biscuits, crushed

400 g/14 oz cream cheese

2 large eggs

140 g/5 oz caster sugar

1½ tsp vanilla essence

450 ml/16 fl oz soured cream

BLUEBERRY TOPPING

55 g/2 oz caster sugar

4 tbsp water

250 g/9 oz fresh blueberries

1 tsp arrowroot

1. Preheat the oven to 190°C/375°F/Gas Mark 5. Brush a 20-cm/8-inch springform tin with oil. Melt the butter in a saucepan over a low heat. Stir in the biscuits, then spread in the tin. Place the cream cheese, eggs, 100 g/3½ oz of the sugar and ½ teaspoon of the vanilla essence in a food processor. Process until smooth. Pour over the biscuit base and smooth the top. Place on a baking tray and bake for 20 minutes, or until set. Remove from the oven and leave to stand for 20 minutes. Leave the oven switched on.

2. Mix the cream with the remaining sugar and vanilla essence in a bowl. Spoon over the cheesecake. Return it to the oven for 10 minutes, leave to cool, then chill in the refrigerator for 8 hours or overnight.

3. To make the topping, place the sugar in a saucepan with half of the water over a low heat and stir until the sugar has dissolved. Increase the heat, add the blueberries, cover and cook for a few minutes, or until they begin to soften. Remove from the heat. Mix the arrowroot and remaining water in a bowl, add to the fruit and stir until smooth. Return to a low heat. Cook until the juice thickens and turns translucent. Leave to cool. Remove the cheesecake from the tin 1 hour before serving. Spoon the fruit on top and chill until ready to serve.

English Muffins

MAKES 10 – 12

2 x 7 g/1/8 oz sachets easy-blend dried yeast

250 ml/9 fl oz tepid water

125 ml/4 fl oz natural yogurt

450 g/1 lb strong plain flour

1/2 tsp salt

50 g/1 3/4 oz fine semolina

oil, for greasing

butter and jam, to serve

1. Mix the yeast with half the tepid water in a bowl until it has dissolved.
2. Add the remaining water and the yogurt and mix well.
3. Sieve the flour into a large bowl and add the salt. Pour in the yeast liquid and mix well to a soft dough.
4. Turn out onto a floured surface and knead well until very smooth. Put the dough back into the bowl, cover with clingfilm and leave to rise for 30–40 minutes in a warm place until it has doubled in size.
5. Turn out again onto the surface and knead lightly. Roll out the dough to a thickness of 2 cm/3/4 inch.
6. Using a 7.5-cm/3-inch cutter, cut into rounds and scatter the semolina over each muffin. Re-roll the trimmings of the dough and make further muffins until it is all used up. Place them on a lightly floured baking tray, cover and allow to rise again for 30–40 minutes.
7. Heat a griddle or a large frying pan and lightly grease with a little oil. Cook half the muffins for 7–8 minutes on each side, taking care not to burn them. Repeat with the rest of the muffins.
8. Serve freshly cooked with lots of butter. Muffins can be kept for 2 days in an airtight tin. To reheat, split them across the centre and quickly toast them before serving with butter and jam.

SERVES 4 – 6

600 ml/1 pint full-fat milk

1 vanilla pod, split

175 g/6 oz caster sugar

4 tbsp water

squeeze of lemon juice

2 large eggs

2 large egg yolks

Crème Caramel

1. Preheat the oven to 160°C/325°F/Gas Mark 3. Lightly grease the sides of a 1.2-litre/2-pint soufflé dish.
2. Pour the milk into a small heavy-based saucepan. Use the tip of a knife to scrape the tiny seeds of the vanilla pod into the milk, then add the vanilla pod. Slowly bring the milk to the boil, then remove the pan from the heat and stir in 85 g/3 oz of the sugar, stirring until it dissolves. Leave to stand for at least 15 minutes to let the vanilla infuse.
3. Place the remaining sugar in another small heavy-based saucepan with the water over a medium heat. Stir until the sugar dissolves, then increase the heat and bring to the boil, without stirring. Continue boiling until the caramel turns a deep golden brown. Watch carefully as it can burn quickly.
4. Immediately squeeze a few drops of lemon juice into the caramel to stop the cooking. Pour the caramel into the prepared soufflé dish and swirl around, so that it coats the base.
5. Bring a kettle of water to the boil. Beat the eggs and egg yolks together. Reheat the milk just until small bubbles appear around the sides, without boiling. Slowly pour the milk into the eggs, whisking constantly.
6. Strain the milk mixture through a fine sieve directly into the prepared soufflé dish and remove the vanilla pod. Transfer the soufflé dish to a roasting tin and pour in enough water to come halfway up the side of the dish.
7. Put the roasting tin in the oven and bake for 75–90 minutes until a knife inserted into the centre of the custard comes out clean. Remove the soufflé dish from the water and leave to cool completely. Cover with clingfilm and leave to chill for at least 24 hours.
8. To serve, run a round-bladed knife around the edge. Invert the Crème Caramel onto a serving dish with a rim, giving a good shake halfway over, then lift off the soufflé dish.

Double Chocolate Brownies

MAKES 9 LARGE OR 16 SMALL

115 g/4 oz butter, plus extra for greasing

115 g/4 oz plain chocolate, broken into pieces

300 g/10½ oz golden caster sugar

pinch of salt

1 tsp vanilla essence

2 large eggs

140 g/5 oz plain flour

2 tbsp cocoa powder

100 g/3½ oz white chocolate chips

FUDGE SAUCE

4 tbsp butter

225 g/8 oz golden caster sugar

150 ml/5 fl oz milk

250 ml/9 fl oz double cream

225 g/8 oz golden syrup

200 g/7 oz plain chocolate, broken into pieces

1. Preheat the oven to 180°C/350°F/Gas Mark 4. Grease and line the bottom of a 18-cm/7-inch square cake tin. Place the butter and chocolate in a small heatproof bowl set over a saucepan of gently simmering water until melted. Stir until smooth. Leave to cool slightly. Stir in the sugar, salt and vanilla essence. Add the eggs, one at a time, until blended.

2. Sift the flour and cocoa powder into the mixture and beat until smooth. Stir in the chocolate chips, then pour the mixture into the tin. Bake in the preheated oven for 35-40 minutes, or until the top is evenly coloured and a cocktail stick inserted into the centre comes out almost clean. Leave to cool slightly while preparing the sauce.

3. To make the sauce, place the butter, sugar, milk, cream and syrup in a small saucepan and heat gently until the sugar has dissolved. Bring to the boil and stir for 10 minutes, or until the mixture is caramel-coloured. Remove from the heat and add the chocolate. Stir until smooth. Cut the brownies into squares and serve immediately with the sauce.

Lemon Meringue Pie

SERVES 4

PASTRY

155 g/5½ oz plain flour, plus extra for dusting

85 g/3 oz butter, cut into small pieces, plus extra for greasing

35 g/1¼ oz icing sugar, sifted

finely grated rind of ½ lemon

½ egg yolk, beaten

1½ tbsp milk

FILLING

3 tbsp cornflour

300 ml/10 fl oz water

juice and grated rind of 2 lemons

175 g/6 oz caster sugar

2 eggs, separated

1. To make the pastry, sift the flour into a bowl. Rub in the butter with the fingertips until the mixture resembles fine breadcrumbs. Mix in the remaining ingredients. Knead briefly on a lightly floured work surface. Rest for 30 minutes.

2. Preheat the oven to 180°C/350°F/Gas Mark 4. Grease a 20-cm/8-inch pie dish with butter. Roll out the pastry to a thickness of 5 mm/¼ inch; use it to line the base and side of the dish. Prick all over with a fork, line with baking paper and fill with baking beans. Bake for 15 minutes. Remove the pastry case from the oven and take out the paper and beans. Reduce the temperature to 150°C/300°F/Gas Mark 2.

3. To make the filling, mix the cornflour with a little of the water. Put the remaining water in a saucepan. Stir in the lemon juice and rind and cornflour paste. Bring to the boil, stirring. Cook for 2 minutes. Cool a little. Stir in 5 tablespoons of the sugar and the egg yolks and pour into the pastry case.

4. Whisk the egg whites in a clean, grease-free bowl until stiff. Gradually whisk in the remaining sugar and spread over the pie. Bake for a further 40 minutes. Remove from oven, cool and serve.

Caramel Chocolate Shortbread

Caramel Chocolate Shortbread

SERVES 12

115 g/4 oz butter, plus extra for greasing

175 g/6 oz plain flour

55 g/2 oz golden caster sugar

200 g/7 oz plain chocolate, broken into pieces

CARAMEL

175 g/6 oz butter

115 g/4 oz golden caster sugar

3 tbsp golden syrup

400 g/14 oz canned condensed milk

1 Preheat the oven to 180°C/350°F/Gas Mark 4. Grease and line the base of a 23-cm/9-inch shallow square cake tin. Place the butter, flour and sugar in a food processor and process until it begins to bind together. Press into the tin and smooth the top. Bake in the oven for 20–25 minutes, or until golden.

2 Meanwhile, make the caramel. Place the butter, sugar, syrup and condensed milk in a heavy-based saucepan. Heat gently until the sugar has melted. Bring to the boil, then reduce the heat and simmer for 6–8 minutes, stirring, until very thick. Pour over the shortbread and chill in the refrigerator for 2 hours, or until firm.

3 Melt the chocolate and leave to cool, then spread over the caramel. Leave to chill in the refrigerator for 2 hours, or until set. Cut the shortbread into 12 pieces using a sharp knife and serve.

Chocolate Fudge Cake

SERVES 8

175 g/6 oz unsalted butter, softened,

plus extra for greasing

175 g/6 oz golden caster sugar

3 eggs, beaten

3 tbsp golden syrup

40 g/1 1/2 oz ground almonds

175 g/6 oz self-raising flour

pinch of salt

40 g/1 1/2 oz cocoa powder

ICING

225 g/8 oz plain chocolate, broken into pieces

55 g/2 oz dark muscovado sugar

225 g/8 oz unsalted butter, diced

5 tbsp evaporated milk

1/2 tsp vanilla essence

1. Grease and line the base of 2 x 20-cm/8-inch cake tins. To make the icing, place the chocolate, sugar, butter, evaporated milk and vanilla essence in a heavy-based saucepan. Heat gently, stirring constantly, until melted. Pour into a bowl and leave to cool. Cover and chill in the refrigerator for 1 hour, or until spreadable.

2. Preheat the oven to 180°C/350°F/Gas Mark 4. Place the butter and sugar in a bowl and beat together until light and fluffy. Gradually beat in the eggs. Stir in the syrup and ground almonds. Sift the flour, salt and cocoa powder into a separate bowl, then fold into the mixture. Add a little water, if necessary, to make a dropping consistency. Spoon the mixture into the prepared tins and bake in the oven for 30-35 minutes, or until springy to the touch and a skewer inserted in the centre comes out clean.

3. Leave the cakes in the tins for 5 minutes, then turn out onto wire racks to cool completely. When the cakes are cold, sandwich them together with half the icing. Spread the remaining icing over the top and sides of the cake, swirling it to give a frosted appearance.

Blueberry & Lemon Drizzle Cake

Blueberry & Lemon Drizzle Cake

SERVES 12

225 g/8 oz butter, softened, plus extra for greasing

225 g/8 oz golden caster sugar

4 eggs, beaten

250 g/9 oz self-raising flour, sifted

finely grated rind and juice of 1 lemon

25 g/1 oz ground almonds

200 g/7 oz fresh blueberries

TOPPING

juice of 2 lemons

115 g/4 oz golden caster sugar

1 Preheat the oven to 180°C/350°F/Gas Mark 4, then grease and line the base of a 20-cm/8-inch square cake tin. Place the butter and sugar in a bowl and beat together until light and fluffy. Gradually beat in the eggs, adding a little flour towards the end to prevent curdling. Beat in the lemon rind, then fold in the remaining flour and almonds with enough of the lemon juice to give a good dropping consistency.

2 Fold in three-quarters of the blueberries and turn into the prepared tin. Smooth the surface, then scatter the remaining blueberries on top. Bake in the preheated oven for 1 hour, or until firm to the touch and a skewer inserted into the centre comes out clean.

3 To make the topping, place the lemon juice and sugar in a bowl and mix together. As soon as the cake comes out of the oven, prick it all over with a fine skewer and pour over the lemon mixture. Leave to cool in the tin until completely cold, then cut into 12 squares to serve.

Jam Roly-Poly

SERVES 6

225 g/8 oz self-raising flour

pinch of salt

115 g/4 oz suet

grated rind of 1 lemon

1 tbsp sugar

125 ml/4 fl oz mixed milk and water

4–6 tbsp strawberry jam

2 tablespoons milk

Custard, to serve

CUSTARD

425ml/15 fl oz single cream

5 egg yolks

3 tbsp caster sugar

1/2 tsp vanilla extract

1 tsp cornflour (optional)

1. Sift the flour into a mixing bowl and add the salt and suet. Mix together well. Stir in the lemon rind and the sugar.
2. Make a well in the centre and add the liquid to give a light, elastic dough. Knead lightly until smooth. If you have time, wrap the dough in clingfilm and leave it to rest for 30 minutes.
3. Roll the dough into a 20 x 25-cm/8 x 10-inch rectangle.
4. Spread the jam over the dough, leaving a 1 cm/1/2 inch border. Brush the border with the milk and roll up the dough carefully, like a Swiss roll, from one short end. Seal the ends.
5. Wrap the roly-poly loosely in greaseproof paper and then in foil, sealing the ends well.
6. Prepare a steamer by half filling it with water and putting it onto boil. Place the roly-poly in the steamer and steam over rapidly boiling water for 1 1/2–2 hours, making sure you top up the water from time to time.
7. To make the custard, heat the cream in a small saucepan just to boiling point. Cream the egg yolks, sugar and vanilla extract together in a measuring jug. You can add the cornflour to this cold egg yolk mixture to ensure the sauce does not separate. Pour the hot cream into the jug, stirring all the time. Return the mixture to the saucepan. Heat the custard very gently, stirring constantly, until the sauce has just thickened, then remove from the heat. Alternatively, you can cook the custard in a bowl over a saucepan of simmering water to prevent overcooking.
8. When cooked, remove from the steamer, unwrap and serve on a warm plate, cut into slices with warm custard.

Chocolate Mousse

SERVES 4 – 6

225 g/8 oz plain chocolate, chopped

2 tbsp brandy, Grand Marnier or Cointreau

4 tbsp water

30 g/1 oz unsalted butter, diced

3 large eggs, separated

1/4 tsp cream of tartar

55 g/2 oz sugar

125 ml/4 fl oz double cream

1. Place the chocolate, brandy and water in a small saucepan over a low heat and melt, stirring, until smooth. Remove the saucepan from the heat and beat in the butter.
2. Beat the egg yolks into the chocolate mixture, one after another, until blended, then leave to cool slightly.
3. Meanwhile, using an electric mixer on low speed, beat the egg whites in a spotlessly clean bowl until they are frothy, then gradually increase the mixer's speed and beat until soft peaks form. Sprinkle the cream of tartar over the surface, then add the sugar, tablespoon by tablespoon, and continue beating until stiff peaks form. Beat several tablespoons of the egg whites into the chocolate mixture to loosen.
4. In another bowl, whip the cream until soft peaks form. Spoon the cream over the chocolate mixture, then spoon the remaining whites over the cream. Use a large metal spoon or rubber spatula to fold the chocolate into the cream and egg whites.
5. Either spoon the chocolate mousse into a large serving bowl or divide it between 4 or 6 individual bowls. Cover the bowl(s) with clingfilm and chill the mousse for at least 3 hours before serving.

Chocolate Chip Ice Cream with Hot Chocolate Fudge Sauce

Chocolate Chip Ice Cream with Hot Chocolate Fudge Sauce

SERVES 4 – 6

300 ml/10 fl oz full-fat milk

1 vanilla pod

115 g/4 oz milk chocolate

85 g/3 oz caster sugar

3 egg yolks

300 ml/10 fl oz whipping cream

CHOCOLATE FUDGE SAUCE

50 g/1¾ oz milk chocolate, broken into pieces

25 g/1 oz butter

4 tbsp full-fat milk

225 g/8 oz soft light brown sugar

2 tbsp golden syrup

1. Pour the milk into a heavy-based saucepan, add the vanilla pod and bring almost to the boil. Remove from the heat and leave to infuse for 30 minutes. Meanwhile, chop the chocolate into small pieces and set aside.

2. Put the sugar and egg yolks in a large bowl and whisk together until pale and the mixture leaves a trail when the whisk is lifted. Remove the vanilla pod from the milk, then slowly add the milk to the sugar mixture, stirring all the time with a wooden spoon. Strain the mixture into the rinsed-out saucepan or a double boiler and cook over a low heat for 10–15 minutes, stirring all the time, until the mixture thickens enough to coat the back of the spoon. Do not boil or it will curdle.

3. Remove the custard from the heat and leave to cool for at least 1 hour, stirring from time to time to prevent a skin from forming. Meanwhile, whip the cream until it holds its shape. Keep in the refrigerator until ready to use.

4. If using an ice cream machine, fold the cold custard into the whipped cream, then churn the mixture in the machine following the manufacturer's instructions. Just before the ice cream freezes, add the chocolate pieces. Alternatively, freeze the custard in a freezerproof container, uncovered, for 1–2 hours, or until it begins to set around the edges. Turn the custard into a bowl and stir with a fork or beat in a food processor until smooth. Fold in the whipped cream and chocolate pieces. Return to the freezer and freeze for a further 2–3 hours, or until firm or required. Cover the container with a lid for storing.

5. Make the chocolate sauce just before you serve the ice cream. Put the chocolate, butter and milk in a heatproof bowl set over a saucepan of simmering water and heat gently, stirring occasionally, until the chocolate has melted and the sauce is smooth. Transfer the mixture to a heavy-based saucepan and stir in the sugar and syrup. Heat gently until the sugar has dissolved, then bring to the boil and boil, without stirring, for 5 minutes. Serve the hot sauce poured over the ice cream.

Carrot Cake

SERVES 8

butter, for greasing

175 g/6 oz light muscovado sugar

3 eggs

175 ml/6 fl oz sunflower oil

175 g/6 oz coarsely grated carrots

2 ripe bananas, mashed

55 g/2 oz walnuts, chopped

280 g/10 oz plain flour

1/2 tsp salt

1 tsp bicarbonate of soda

2 tsp baking powder

FROSTING

200 g/7 oz cream cheese

1/2 tsp vanilla essence

115 g/4 oz icing sugar

25 g/1 oz walnuts, chopped

1. Preheat the oven to 180°C/350°F/Gas Mark 4. Grease and line the base of a 23-cm/9-inch springform cake tin. Place the sugar, eggs, sunflower oil, carrots, bananas and walnuts in a bowl. Sift in the flour, salt, bicarbonate of soda and baking powder. Beat the mixture until smooth.

2. Turn the mixture into the prepared tin and bake in the preheated oven for 1 hour 5 minutes, or until well risen and golden brown and a skewer inserted into the centre comes out clean. Leave in the tin for 10 minutes, then turn out and peel off the lining paper. Transfer to a wire rack to cool completely.

3. To make the frosting, place the cream cheese and vanilla essence in a bowl and beat well to soften. Beat in the icing sugar a tablespoon at a time, until smooth. Swirl over the cake and sprinkle the chopped walnuts on top. Leave in a cool place for the frosting to harden slightly before serving.

Trifle

SERVES 6 – 8

8 trifle sponges

115 g/4 oz raspberry jam

150 ml/¼ pint sherry

55 g/2 oz small macaroons or ratafia biscuits

2 tbsp brandy

350 g/12 oz raspberries, fresh or frozen

568 ml/1 pint Custard (see page 38), cooled

300 ml/½ pint double cream

2 tbsp milk

40 g/1½ oz toasted flaked almonds or silver dragées, to decorate

1. Break the sponges or cake into pieces and spread with the jam.
2. Place in a large glass serving bowl and pour over the sherry.
3. Add the macaroons to the bowl and sprinkle over the brandy.
4. Spoon the raspberries on top.
5. Pour over the Custard, cover the bowl with clingfilm and leave to settle for 2–3 hours or overnight.
6. Just before serving, whip the cream with the milk until it is thick but still soft. Spoon over the custard and swirl around using a knife to give an attractive appearance. Decorate as desired with almonds or dragées and serve chilled.

Deep Chocolate Cheesecake

SERVES 4 – 6

BASE

4 tbsp butter, melted, plus extra for greasing

115 g/4 oz digestive biscuits, finely crushed

2 tsp unsweetened cocoa powder

CHOCOLATE LAYER

800 g/1 lb 12 oz mascarpone cheese

200 g/7 oz icing sugar, sifted

juice of 1/2 orange

finely grated rind of 1 orange

175 g/6 oz dark chocolate, melted

2 tbsp brandy

Chocolate Leaves and halved kumquats, to decorate

CHOCOLATE LEAVES

75g/2 3/4 oz dark chocolate, melted

handful of rose leaves, or other small edible leaves with well-defined veins, washed and dried

1 Grease a 20-cm/8-inch loose-bottomed cake tin.

2 To make the base, put the crushed biscuits, cocoa powder and melted butter into a large bowl and mix well. Press the biscuit mixture evenly over the base of the prepared tin.

3 Put the mascarpone and sugar into a bowl and stir in the orange juice and rind. Add the melted chocolate and brandy, and mix together until thoroughly combined. Spread the chocolate mixture evenly over the biscuit layer. Cover with clingfilm and chill for at least 4 hours.

4 To make the leaves, brush the melted chocolate over the bottom of the leaves. Arrange, coated sides up, on a baking sheet lined with baking paper. Chill until set, then peel the leaves away.

5 Remove the cheesecake from the refrigerator, turn out onto a serving platter and decorate with Chocolate Leaves and kumquat halves. Serve immediately.

Chocolate & Cherry Tiramisù

SERVES 4

200 ml/7 fl oz strong black coffee, cooled to room temperature

6 tbsp cherry brandy

16 trifle sponges

250 g/9 oz mascarpone

300 ml/10 fl oz double cream, lightly whipped

3 tbsp icing sugar

275 g/9½ oz sweet cherries, halved and stoned

60 g/2¼ oz chocolate, curls or grated

whole cherries, to decorate

1. Pour the cooled coffee into a jug and stir in the cherry brandy. Put half of the trifle sponges into the bottom of a serving dish, then pour over half of the coffee mixture.

2. Put the mascarpone into a separate bowl along with the cream and sugar and mix together well. Spread half of the mascarpone mixture over the coffee-soaked trifle sponges, then top with half of the cherries. Arrange the remaining trifle sponges on top. Pour over the remaining coffee mixture and top with the remaining cherries. Finish with a layer of mascarpone mixture. Scatter over the grated chocolate, cover with clingfilm, and chill in the refrigerator for at least 2 hours.

3. Remove from the refrigerator, decorate with cherries and serve.

Soothing Savoury

Soothing Savoury

Bubbling, steaming, warming and oh so comforting, these tasty dishes are sure to soothe and satisfy. From traditional heart-warming casseroles and stews to delicious Friday-night fare such as pizza or spare ribs, these Soothing Savoury dishes have an answer for every day of the week.

Roasted Tomato Soup

Roasted Tomato Soup

SERVES 4 – 6

900 g/2 lb large, juicy tomatoes, halved

2 tbsp butter

1 tbsp olive oil

1 large onion, sliced

2–3 tbsp tomato purée, depending on the flavour of the tomatoes

900 ml/1½ pints vegetable stock

2 tbsp amontillado sherry

½ tsp sugar

salt and pepper

crusty bread, to serve

soured cream and parsley, to garnish

1. Preheat the grill to high. Place the tomatoes, cut sides up, on a baking sheet and grill about 10 cm/4 inches from the heat for 5 minutes, or until just starting to char on the edges.

2. Meanwhile, melt the butter with the oil in a large saucepan or flameproof casserole over a medium heat. Add the onion and fry for 5 minutes, stirring occasionally. Stir in the tomato purée and continue frying for about two minutes.

3. Add the tomatoes, stock, sherry, sugar and salt and pepper to taste to the saucepan and stir. Bring to the boil, then reduce the heat to low and simmer, covered, for about 20 minutes until the tomatoes are reduced to a pulp.

4. Process the soup through a food processor into a large bowl. Return to the rinsed saucepan and reheat, uncovered, simmering 10 minutes, or until the desired consistency is achieved. Ladle into individual bowls and serve with plenty of bread. Garnish with a swirl of soured cream (1tbsp per bowl) and sprinkle with parsley.

Sausages & Mash with Onion Gravy

SERVES 4

8 good-quality sausages

1 tbsp oil

FOR THE ONION GRAVY

3 onions, cut in half and thinly sliced

70 g/2½ oz butter

125 ml/4 fl oz Marsala or port

125 ml/4 fl oz vegetable stock

salt and pepper

FOR THE MASHED POTATO

900 g/2 lb floury potatoes, such as King Edwards, Maris Piper or Desirée, peeled and cut into chunks

salt and pepper

55 g/2 oz butter

3 tbsp hot milk

2 tbsp chopped fresh parsley

1. Cook the sausages slowly in a frying pan with the oil over a low heat. Cover the pan and turn the sausages from time to time. Don't rush the cooking, because you want them well-cooked and sticky. They will take 25–30 minutes.

2. Meanwhile, prepare the onion gravy by placing the onion in a frying pan with the butter and frying over a low heat until soft, stirring continuously. Continue to cook until they are brown and almost melting, stirring from time to time. This will take about 30 minutes, but it is worth it as the onions will naturally caramelize.

3. Pour in the Marsala and stock and continue to bubble away until the onion gravy is really thick. Season with salt and pepper to taste.

4. To make the mashed potato, cook the potatoes in a large saucepan of boiling salted water for 15–20 minutes. Drain well and mash with a potato masher until smooth. Season with salt and pepper, add the butter, milk and parsley and stir well.

5. Serve the sausages really hot with the mashed potato and the onion gravy spooned over the top.

Cheese & Tomato Pizza

Cheese & Tomato Pizza

SERVES 2

FOR THE DOUGH

225 g/8 oz plain flour, plus extra for dusting

1 tsp salt

1 tsp easy-blend dried yeast

1 tbsp olive oil, plus extra for brushing

6 tbsp lukewarm water

FOR THE TOPPING

6 tomatoes, sliced thinly

175 g/6 oz mozzarella cheese, drained and sliced thinly

salt and pepper

2 tbsp shredded fresh basil leaves

2 tbsp olive oil

1. To make the pizza dough, sift the flour and salt into a bowl and stir in the yeast. Make a well in the centre and pour in the oil and water. Gradually incorporate the dry ingredients into the liquid, using a wooden spoon or floured hands.

2. Turn out the dough onto a lightly floured surface and knead well for 5 minutes, until smooth and elastic. Return to the clean bowl, covered with lightly oiled clingfilm and set aside to rise in a warm place for about 1 hour, or until doubled in size.

3. Turn out the dough onto a lightly floured surface and knock back. Knead briefly, then cut it in half and roll out each piece into a round about 5 mm/1/4 inch thick. Transfer to a lightly oiled baking sheet and push up the edges with your fingers to form a small rim.

4. For the topping, arrange the tomato and mozzarella slices alternately over the pizza bases. Season to taste with salt and pepper, sprinkle with the basil and drizzle with the olive oil.

5. Bake in a preheated oven, 230°C/450°F/Gas Mark 8, for 15–20 minutes, until the crust is crisp and the cheese has melted. Serve immediately.

Creamy Leek Bake

SERVES 4

55 g/2 oz unsalted butter, melted

115 g/4 oz ground almonds

55 g/2 oz toasted chopped hazelnuts

25 g/1 oz sesame seeds

85 g/3 oz mature Cheddar cheese, grated

1 tbsp virgin olive oil

350 g/12 oz leeks, thinly sliced

1 large red pepper, skinned, deseeded and cut into strips

1 orange pepper, skinned, deseeded and cut into strips

85 g/3 oz button mushrooms, sliced

250 g/9 oz crème fraîche

1 tbsp chopped fresh oregano

salt and pepper

1. Preheat the oven to 190°C/375°F/Gas Mark 5. Mix the butter, nuts, sesame seeds and half the cheese together in a bowl. Press the mixture into the base of an 850-ml/1½-pint ovenproof gratin dish. Bake in the preheated oven for 15 minutes, or until the top is golden.

2. Meanwhile, heat the oil in a large frying pan over a medium heat, add the leeks, peppers and mushrooms and cook for 5 minutes, stirring occasionally. Stir in the crème fraîche, oregano and salt and pepper to taste.

3. Remove the nut base from the oven. Spread the crème fraîche mixture over the nut base and sprinkle with the remaining cheese. Bake in the oven for 15–20 minutes, or until the cheese is golden brown and bubbling.

Italian Steak Melt Burgers

Italian Steak Melt Burgers

SERVES 4

450 g/1 lb best steak mince

1 onion, grated

2–4 garlic cloves, crushed

1 small red pepper, deseeded, peeled and chopped

55 g/2 oz stoned black olives, finely chopped

pepper

1 tbsp tomato purée

2 large tomatoes, thickly sliced

85 g/3 oz Gruyère cheese, sliced

ciabatta rolls, rocket leaves, balsamic vinegar, to serve

Parmesan cheese shavings, to garnish

1. Place the steak mince, onion, garlic, red pepper, olives, pepper and tomato purée in a food processor and, using the pulse button, blend together. Shape into 4 equal-sized burgers, then cover and leave to chill for at least 30 minutes.

2. Preheat the grill to medium-high. Place the burgers on a foil-lined grill rack and cook under the hot grill for 3–5 minutes on each side or until cooked to personal preference.

3. Place a tomato slice on top of each burger, then place the cheese over the tomato. Grill for a further 2–3 minutes, or until the cheese begins to melt. Serve.

4. Place some rocket leaves on the bases of 4 lightly toasted ciabatta rolls and drizzle with a little balsamic vinegar. Place the burgers on top, garnish with Parmesan cheese shavings. Place the lid in position and serve.

Spaghetti with Meatballs

SERVES 6

1 potato, diced

400 g/14 oz minced steak

1 onion, finely chopped

1 egg

4 tbsp chopped fresh flat-leaf parsley

plain flour, for dusting

5 tbsp virgin olive oil

400 ml/14 fl oz passata

2 tbsp tomato purée

400 g/14 oz dried spaghetti

salt and pepper

6 fresh basil leaves, shredded freshly and

grated Parmesan, to garnish

1. Place the potato in a small pan, add cold water to cover and a pinch of salt and bring to the boil. Cook for 10–15 minutes, until tender, then drain. Either mash thoroughly with a potato masher or fork or pass through a potato dicer.

2. Combine the potato, steak, onion, egg and parsley in a bowl and season to taste with salt and pepper. Spread out the flour on a plate. With dampened hands, shape the meat mixture into walnut-size balls and roll in the flour. Shake off any excess.

3. Heat the oil in a heavy-based frying pan, add the meatballs and cook over a medium heat, stirring and turning frequently, for 8–10 minutes, until golden all over.

4. Add the passata and tomato purée and cook for a further 10 minutes, until the sauce is reduced and thickened.

5. Meanwhile, bring a large saucepan of lightly salted water to the boil. Add the pasta, bring back to the boil and cook for 8-10 minutes, until tender, but still firm to the bite.

6. Drain well and add to the meatball sauce, tossing well to coat. Transfer to a warm serving dish, garnish with the basil leaves and Parmesan and serve immediately.

Oven-Baked Risotto With Mushrooms

SERVES 4

1.3 litres/2¼ pints chicken or vegetable stock

4 tbsp olive oil

400 g/14 oz portobello or large field mushrooms, thickly sliced

115 g/4 oz pancetta or thick-cut smoked bacon, diced

1 large onion, finely chopped

2 garlic cloves, finely chopped

350 g/12 oz risotto rice

2 tbsp chopped fresh tarragon or flat-leaf parsley

85 g/3 oz freshly grated Parmesan cheese, plus extra for sprinkling

salt and pepper

1. Preheat the oven to 180°C/350°F/Gas Mark 4. Bring the stock to the boil in a saucepan, then reduce the heat and keep simmering gently over a low heat while you are cooking the risotto.
2. Heat half the oil in a large, heavy-based frying pan over a high heat. Add the mushrooms and stir-fry for 2–3 minutes until golden and tender-crisp. Transfer to a plate.
3. Add the pancetta to the frying pan and cook, stirring frequently, for 2 minutes, or until crisp and golden. Remove with a slotted spoon and add to the mushrooms on the plate.
4. Heat the remaining oil in a large, heavy-based saucepan over a medium heat. Add the onion and cook, stirring occasionally, for 2 minutes. Add the garlic and cook for 1 minute.
5. Reduce the heat, add the rice and mix to coat in oil. Cook, stirring constantly, for 2–3 minutes, or until the grains are translucent.
6. Gradually stir the hot stock into the rice, then add the mushroom and pancetta mixture and the tarragon. Season to taste with salt and pepper. Bring to the boil.
7. Remove the saucepan from the heat and transfer the mixture to a casserole or an ovenproof dish.
8. Cover and bake in the oven for 20 minutes, or until the rice is almost tender and most of the liquid is absorbed. Uncover and stir in the Parmesan. Continue to bake for a further 15 minutes until the rice is creamy. Serve immediately with extra Parmesan for sprinkling.

Fisherman's Pie

SERVES 6

butter, for greasing

900 g/2 lb white fish fillets, such as plaice, skinned

salt and pepper

150 ml/$^{1}/_{4}$ pint dry white wine

1 tbsp chopped fresh parsley, tarragon or dill

175 g/6 oz small mushrooms, sliced

110 g/3$^{1}/_{2}$ oz butter

175 g/6 oz cooked peeled prawns

40 g/1$^{1}/_{2}$ oz plain flour

125 ml/4 fl oz double cream

900 g/2 lb floury potatoes, such as King Edwards, Maris Piper or Desirée, peeled and cut into chunks

1. Preheat the oven to 180°C/350°F/Gas Mark 4. Butter a 1.7-litre/3-pint baking dish.
2. Fold the fish fillets in half and place in the dish. Season well with salt and pepper, pour over the wine and scatter over the herbs.
3. Cover with foil and bake for 15 minutes until the fish starts to flake. Strain off the liquid and reserve for the sauce. Increase the oven temperature to 220°C/425°F/Gas Mark 7.
4. Sauté the mushrooms in a frying pan with 15 g/$^{1}/_{2}$ oz of the butter and spoon over the fish. Scatter over the prawns.
5. Heat 55 g/2 oz of the butter in a saucepan and stir in the flour. Cook for a few minutes without browning, remove from the heat, then add the reserved cooking liquid gradually, stirring well between each addition.
6. Return to the heat and gently bring to the boil, still stirring to ensure a smooth sauce. Add the cream and season to taste with salt and pepper. Pour over the fish in the dish and smooth over the surface.
7. Make the mashed potato by cooking the potatoes in boiling salted water for 15–20 minutes. Drain well and mash with a potato masher until smooth. Season to taste with salt and pepper and add the remaining butter, stirring until melted.
8. Pile or pipe the potato onto the fish and sauce and bake for 10–15 minutes until golden brown.

Tagliatelle with a Rich Meat Sauce

SERVES 4

4 tbsp olive oil, plus extra for serving

85 g/3 oz pancetta or rindless streaky bacon, diced

1 onion, chopped

1 garlic clove, chopped finely

1 carrot, chopped

1 celery stick, chopped

225 g/8 oz minced steak

115 g/4 oz chicken livers, chopped

2 tbsp passata

125 ml/4 fl oz dry white wine

225 ml/8 fl oz beef stock or water

1 tbsp chopped fresh oregano

1 bay leaf

salt and pepper

450 g/1 lb dried tagliatelle

freshly grated Parmesan cheese, to serve

1. Heat the olive oil in a large, heavy-based saucepan. Add the pancetta or bacon and cook over a medium heat, stirring occasionally, for 3–5 minutes, until it is just turning brown. Add the onion, garlic, carrot and celery and cook, stirring occasionally, for a further 5 minutes.

2. Add the steak and cook over a high heat, breaking up the meat with a wooden spoon, for 5 minutes, until browned. Stir in the chicken livers and cook, stirring occasionally, for a further 2–3 minutes. Add the passata, wine, stock, oregano and bay leaf and season to taste with salt and pepper. Bring to the boil, lower the heat, cover and simmer for 30–35 minutes.

3. When the sauce is almost cooked, bring a large saucepan of lightly salted water to the boil. Add the pasta, bring back to the boil and cook for 8–10 minutes, until tender, but still firm to the bite. Drain, transfer to a warmed serving dish, drizzle with a little olive oil and toss well.

4. Remove and discard the bay leaf from the sauce, then pour it over the pasta, toss again and serve immediately with grated Parmesan.

Spare Ribs

SERVES 4

900 g/2 lb pork spare ribs

2 tbsp dark soy sauce

3 tbsp hoisin sauce

1 tbsp Chinese rice wine or dry sherry

pinch of Chinese five spice powder

2 tsp dark brown sugar

1/4 tsp chilli sauce

2 garlic cloves, crushed, to garnish

coriander sprigs, to serve

1. Cut the spare ribs into separate pieces if they are joined together. If desired, you can chop them into 5 cm/2-inch lengths, using a cleaver.
2. Mix together the soy sauce, hoisin sauce, Chinese rice wine or sherry, Chinese five spice powder, dark brown sugar, chilli sauce and garlic in a large bowl.
3. Place the ribs in a shallow dish and pour the mixture over them, turning to coat them well. Cover and marinate in the refrigerator, turning the ribs from time to time, for at least 1 hour.
4. Remove the ribs from the marinade and arrange them in a single layer on a wire rack placed over a roasting tin half filled with warm water. Brush with the marinade, reserving the remainder.
5. Cook in a preheated oven, at 180°C/350°F/Gas Mark 4, for 30 minutes. Remove the roasting tin from the oven and turn the ribs over. Brush with the remaining marinade and return to the oven for a further 30 minutes, or until cooked through. Transfer to a warmed serving dish, garnish with the coriander sprigs and serve immediately.

Courgette Pie

SERVES 6 – 8

2 tbsp olive oil

2 bunches spring onions, sliced thinly

50 g/1$^3/_4$ oz arborio or other short-grain rice

175 ml/6 fl oz hot vegetable or chicken stock

750 g/1lb 10 oz courgettes, grated coarsely and left to drain in a colander for 5–10 mins

4 tbsp chopped fresh flat-leaf parsley

2 tbsp chopped fresh mint

3 eggs, beaten

300 g/3$^1/_2$ oz authentic Greek feta cheese

salt and pepper

100 g/3$^1/_2$ oz butter

200 g/7 oz authentic Greek filo pastry

1. Heat the oil in a saucepan, add the spring onions and fry for 5 minutes, until softened. Add the rice and cook for 1 minute, stirring to coat in the oil.
2. Add the stock to the saucepan and simmer for about 15 minutes until the stock has been absorbed and the rice is tender but still firm to the bite. Remove the saucepan from the heat and stir in the courgettes. Leave to cool.
3. When the mixture has cooled, add the parsley, mint and eggs. Crumble in the cheese, season with salt and pepper and mix well together.
4. Melt the butter and use a little to lightly grease a deep 30 x 20 cm/12 x 8 inch roasting tin.
5. Cut the pastry sheets in half widthways. Take 1 sheet of pastry and cover the remaining sheets with a damp tea towel. Use to line the base and sides of the tin and brush the sheet with a little of the melted butter. Repeat with half of the pastry sheets, brushing each with butter.
6. Spread the courgette mixture over the pastry, then top with the remaining pastry sheets, brushing each with butter and tucking down the edges. Using a sharp knife, score the top layers of the pastry into 6–8 squares.
7. Bake the pie in a preheated oven, 190°C/375°F/Gas Mark 5, for about 35 minutes, until golden brown. Serve hot.

Roasted Vegetable Moussaka

SERVES 4 – 6

1 large aubergine

salt

2 medium courgettes, sliced thickly

2 onions, cut into small wedges

2 red peppers, cored, seeded and chopped roughly

2 garlic cloves, chopped roughly

5 tbsp olive oil

1 tbsp chopped fresh thyme

pepper

2 eggs, beaten

300 ml/½ pint authentic Greek yogurt

400 g/14 oz canned chopped tomatoes in juice

55 g/2 oz authentic Greek feta cheese

1. Cut the aubergine into slices, about 5 mm/¼ inch thick. Put in a colander, standing over a large plate, and sprinkle each layer with salt. Cover with a plate and place a heavy weight on top. Leave for 30 minutes to degorge.

2. Rinse the aubergine slices under cold running water, then pat dry with kitchen paper.

3. Put the aubergine, courgettes, onions, peppers and garlic in a roasting tin. Drizzle over the oil, toss together and then sprinkle over the thyme and season with salt and pepper. Roast in a preheated oven, 220°C/425°F/Gas Mark 7, for 30–35 minutes, turning half-way through the cooking, until golden brown and tender.

4. Meanwhile, beat together the eggs, yogurt, salt and pepper. When the vegetables are cooked, reduce the oven temperature to 180°C/350°F/Gas Mark 4.

5. Put half the vegetables in a layer in a large ovenproof dish. Spoon over the canned chopped tomatoes and their juice then add the remaining vegetables. Pour over the yogurt mixture and crumble over the feta cheese. Bake in the oven for 45 minutes–1 hour, until golden brown. Serve hot, warm or cold.

Coq Au Vin

SERVES 4 – 6

1 chicken, weighing 1.6 kg/3 lb 8 oz, cut into 8 pieces

2 tbsp plain flour

85 g/3 oz butter

2 tbsp olive oil

125 g/4½ oz smoked lardons, blanched for 30 seconds, drained and patted dry

12 shallots, peeled but left whole

4 tbsp brandy

2 large garlic cloves, finely chopped

1 Bouquet Garni

1 tbsp tomato purée

1 tsp caster sugar

1 bottle of dry red wine, such as Beaujolais

12 button mushrooms

salt and pepper

sprigs of fresh flat-leaf parsley, to garnish

Fried Croûtes, to serve

FOR THE BEURRE MANIÉ

15 g/½ oz butter, softened

15 g/½ oz plain flour

1 Put the chicken pieces and flour with salt and pepper to taste in a polythene bag, hold the top closed and shake until the chicken pieces are lightly coated all over. Remove the chicken from the bag, shake off any excess flour and set aside.

2 Melt 55 g/2 oz of the butter with 1 tablespoon of the oil in a large sauté or frying pan with a tight-fitting lid or a flameproof casserole over a medium-high heat. Add the lardons and fry for 1 minute. Remove them from the pan with a slotted spoon and set aside.

3 Add the chicken pieces to the pan, skin-side down, and fry for 3–5 minutes until golden brown. Turn the chicken pieces over and continue frying to brown on the other side. Work in batches, if necessary, to avoid overcrowding the pan.

4 Remove the chicken pieces from the pan and set aside. Pour off all but 2 tablespoons of the fat. Add the shallots and sauté them for 3–5 minutes until they are golden on all sides. Transfer to the plate with the lardons and set aside.

5 Return all the chicken pieces to the pan and remove the pan from the heat. Warm the brandy in a ladle or small saucepan, ignite and pour it over the chicken pieces to flambé.

6 When the flames die down, return the pan to the heat, add the garlic, Bouquet Garni, tomato purée, sugar and reserved lardons and shallots and pour in the wine. Bring to the boil, scraping any sediment from the base of the pan.

7 Reduce the heat to low, cover the pan tightly and simmer for 40–45 minutes until the chicken is tender and the juices run clear when a skewer is inserted into the thickest part of the meat.

8 Meanwhile, preheat the oven to its lowest temperature. To make the beurre manié, mash the butter and flour together to make a thick paste and set aside.

9 Melt the remaining butter with the remaining oil in another sauté or frying pan over a medium-high heat. Add the mushrooms, season with salt and pepper to taste and sauté them until they are golden. Remove them from the pan and set aside.

10 Remove the chicken pieces from the pan and keep them warm with the mushrooms in the oven. Discard the Bouquet Garni. Tilt the pan and use a large metal spoon to remove the fat from the surface of the cooking liquid, then bring the cooking liquid to the boil and boil for 3 minutes to reduce.

11 Add small amounts of the beurre manié to the boiling liquid, whisking constantly and only adding more when the previous amount has been incorporated. Continue boiling and whisking until the sauce is thick and shiny. Taste, and adjust the seasoning if necessary. Spoon the sauce over the chicken pieces and mushrooms. Garnish with parsley sprigs and serve immediately with the Fried Croûtes.

Baked Lasagne

SERVES 4

FOR THE MEAT SAUCE

3 tbsp olive oil

1 onion, chopped finely

1 celery stick, chopped finely

1 carrot, chopped finely

100 g/3½ oz pancetta or rindless streaky bacon, chopped finely

175 g/6 oz minced beef

175 g/6 oz minced pork

100 ml/3½ fl oz dry red wine

150 ml/¼ pint beef stock

1 tbsp tomato purée

salt and pepper

1 clove

1 bay leaf

150 ml/¼ pint boiling milk

FOR THE BÉCHAMEL SAUCE

55 g/2 oz unsalted butter

55 g/2 oz plain flour

500 ml/18 fl oz milk

1 bay leaf

salt and pepper

pinch of freshly grated nutmeg

400 g/14 oz dried lasagne verdi

140 g/5 oz mozzarella cheese, drained and diced

140 g/5 oz freshly grated Parmesan cheese

55 g/2 oz unsalted butter, diced, plus extra for greasing

1. First, make the meat sauce. Heat the olive oil in a large, heavy-based saucepan. Add the onion, celery, carrot, pancetta, beef and pork and cook over a medium heat, stirring frequently and breaking up the meat with a wooden spoon, for 10 minutes, until lightly browned.

2. Add the wine, bring to the boil and cook until reduced. Add about two-thirds of the stock, bring to the boil and cook until reduced. Combine the remaining stock and tomato purée and add to the saucepan. Season to taste, add the clove and the bay leaf and pour in the milk. Cover and simmer over a low heat for 1½ hours.

3. Next, make the béchamel sauce. Melt the butter, add the flour and cook over a low heat, stirring constantly, for 1 minute. Remove the saucepan from the heat and gradually stir in the milk. Return the saucepan to the heat and bring to the boil, stirring constantly, until thickened and smooth. Add the bay leaf and simmer gently for 2 minutes. Remove the bay leaf and season the sauce to taste with salt, pepper and nutmeg. Remove the saucepan from the heat and set aside.

4. Unless you are using lasagne that needs no precooking, bring a large saucepan of lightly salted water to the boil. Add the lasagne sheets, in batches, bring back to the boil and cook for about 10 minutes, until tender, but still firm to the bite. Remove with tongs and spread out on a clean tea towel.

5. Remove the meat sauce from the heat and discard the clove and bay leaf. Lightly grease a large, oven-proof dish with butter. Place a layer of lasagne in the base and cover it with a layer of meat sauce. Spoon a layer of béchamel sauce on top and sprinkle with one-third of the mozzarella and Parmesan cheeses. Continue making layers until all the ingredients are used, ending with a topping of béchamel sauce and sprinkled cheese.

6. Dot the top of the lasagne with the diced butter and bake in a preheated oven, 200°C/400°F/Gas Mark 6, for 30 minutes, until golden and bubbling.

Shepherd's Pie

SERVES 8

1 tbsp olive oil

2 onions, finely chopped

2 garlic cloves, finely chopped

675 g/1 lb 8 oz good-quality fresh lamb mince

2 carrots, finely chopped

1 tbsp plain flour

225 ml/8 fl oz beef or chicken stock, plus extra if necessary

125 ml/4 fl oz red wine

Worcestershire sauce

salt and pepper

FOR THE MASHED POTATO

675 g/1 lb 8 oz floury potatoes, such as King Edward, Maris Piper or Desirée, cut into chunks

55 g/2 oz butter

2 tbsp cream or milk

1. Preheat the oven to 180°C/350°F/Gas Mark 4.
2. Heat the oil in a large casserole and fry the onion until softened, then add the garlic and stir well.
3. Increase the heat and add the meat. Cook quickly to brown the meat all over, stirring constantly. Add the carrot and season well with salt and pepper.
4. Stir in the flour and add the stock and wine. Stir well and heat until simmering and thickened.
5. Cover the casserole and cook in the preheated oven for about 1 hour. Check the consistency occasionally and add a little more stock if required. The mixture should be quite thick but not dry. Season to taste with salt and pepper and add a little Worcestershire sauce, if desired.
6. While the meat is cooking, make the mashed potato. Cook the potatoes in a large saucepan of lightly salted boiling water for 15–20 minutes. Drain well and mash with a potato masher until smooth. Add the butter and cream and season well with salt and pepper.
7. Spoon the lamb mixture into an ovenproof serving dish and spread or pipe the potato on top.
8. Increase the oven temperature to 200°C/400°F/Gas Mark 6 and cook the pie for 15–20 minutes at the top of the oven until golden brown. You might like to finish it off under a medium-hot grill for a really crisp brown topping to the potato.

Cheese Gratin

SERVES 4 – 6

900 g/2 lb waxy potatoes, such as Charlotte, peeled and thinly sliced

1 large garlic clove, halved

225 ml/8 fl oz double cream

freshly grated nutmeg

175 g/6 oz Gruyère cheese, finely grated

butter, for greasing and dotting over the top

salt and pepper

1. Preheat the oven to 190°C/375°F/Gas Mark 5. Put the potato slices in a bowl, cover with cold water and leave to stand for 5 minutes, then drain well.

2. Meanwhile, rub the base and sides of a 1.4-litre/ 2½-pint oval gratin or ovenproof dish with the cut sides of the garlic halves, pressing down firmly to impart the flavour. Lightly grease the sides of the dish with butter.

3. Place the potatoes in a bowl with the cream and season to taste with freshly grated nutmeg and salt and pepper. Use your hands to mix everything together, then transfer the potatoes to the gratin dish and pour over any cream remaining in the bowl.

4. Sprinkle the cheese over the top and dot with butter. Place the gratin dish on a baking tray and bake for 60–80 minutes until the potatoes are tender when pierced with a skewer and the top is golden and bubbling. Leave to stand for about 2 minutes, then serve straight from the gratin dish.

Winter Beef Stew with Herb Dumplings

SERVES 4

3 tbsp plain flour

salt and pepper

800 g/1 lb 12 oz braising steak, cubed

3 tbsp olive oil

12 shallots, peeled and halved, or quartered if large

2 carrots, cut into batons

1 parsnip, sliced into rounds

2 bay leaves

1 tbsp chopped fresh rosemary

450 ml/16 fl oz cider

250 ml/16 fl oz beef stock

1 tbsp tamari (soy sauce)

200 g/7 oz canned chestnuts, drained

FOR THE HERB DUMPLINGS

115 g/4 oz self-raising flour, plus extra for flouring

50 g/1¾ oz vegetable suet

2 tbsp chopped fresh thyme

salt and pepper

1. Preheat the oven to 160°C/325°F/Gas Mark 3. Put the flour into a clean polythene bag or on a plate and season generously with salt and pepper. Toss the beef in the seasoned flour until coated.

2. Heat 1 tablespoon of the oil in a large, flameproof casserole dish over a medium-high heat. Add one-third of the beef and cook for 5–6 minutes, turning occasionally, until browned all over – the meat may stick to the pan until it is properly sealed. Remove the beef with a slotted spoon. Cook the remaining 2 batches, adding another tablespoon of oil as necessary. Set aside when all the beef has been sealed.

3. Add the remaining oil to the pan with the shallots, carrots, parsnip and herbs and cook for 3 minutes, stirring occasionally. Pour in the cider and beef stock and bring to the boil. Cook over a high heat until the alcohol has evaporated and the liquid reduced. Add the stock and tamari, then cook for a further 3 minutes.

4. Stir in the chestnuts and beef, cover and cook in the preheated oven for 1 hour 35 minutes.

5. Meanwhile, to make the dumplings, combine all the ingredients in a bowl and season to taste with salt and pepper. Mix in enough water to make a soft dough. Divide the dough into walnut-sized pieces and, using floured hands, roll each piece into a ball.

6. Add to the casserole dish, cover and cook for a further 25 minutes, or until the dumplings are cooked, the stock has formed a thick, rich gravy and the meat is tender. Season to taste with salt and pepper before serving.

Baked Potatoes with Pesto

Baked Potatoes with Pesto

SERVES 4

- 4 baking potatoes, about 225 g/8 oz each
- 150 ml/1/4 pint double cream
- 75 ml/3 fl oz vegetable stock
- 1 tbsp lemon juice
- 2 garlic cloves, crushed
- 3 tbsp chopped basil
- 2 tbsp pine nuts
- 2 tbsp grated Parmesan cheese
- salt and pepper

1. Scrub the potatoes well and prick the skins with a fork. Rub a little salt into the skins and place on a baking tray.
2. Cook in a preheated oven, 190°C/ 375°F/Gas Mark 5, for 1 hour, or until the potatoes are cooked through and the skins are crisp.
3. Remove the potatoes from the oven and cut them in half lengthways. Using a spoon, scoop the potato flesh into a mixing bowl, leaving a thin shell of potato inside the skins. Mash the potato flesh with a fork.
4. Meanwhile, mix the cream and stock in a saucepan and simmer over a low heat for about 8-10 minutes, or until reduced by half.
5. Stir in the lemon juice, garlic and chopped basil and season to taste with salt and pepper. Stir the mixture into the mashed potato flesh, together with the pine nuts.
6. Spoon the mixture back into the potato shells and sprinkle the Parmesan cheese on top. Return the potatoes to the oven for 10 minutes, or until the cheese has browned. Serve.

Chicken Fajitas

SERVES 4

3 tbsp olive oil, plus extra for drizzling

3 tbsp maple syrup or clear honey

1 tbsp red wine vinegar

2 garlic cloves, crushed

2 tsp dried oregano

1–2 tsp dried red chilli flakes

salt and pepper

4 chicken breasts, skinless, boneless

2 red peppers, deseeded and cut into 2.5-cm/1-inch strips

8 floured tortillas, warmed

guacamole, soured cream, salsa and iceberg lettuce, to serve

1. Place the oil, maple syrup, vinegar, garlic, oregano, chilli flakes and salt and pepper to taste in a large, shallow dish or bowl and mix together.

2. Slice the chicken across the grain into slices 2.5 cm/1 inch thick. Toss in the marinade until well coated. Cover and leave to chill in the refrigerator for 2–3 hours, turning occasionally.

3. Heat a griddle pan until hot. Lift the chicken slices from the marinade with a slotted spoon, lay on the griddle pan and cook over medium-high heat for 3–4 minutes on each side, or until cooked through. Remove the chicken to a warmed serving plate and keep warm.

4. Add the peppers, skin side down, to the griddle pan and cook for 2 minutes on each side. Transfer to the serving plate.

5. Serve immediately with the warmed tortillas to be used as wraps. Serve accompaniments separately.

Sausage & Bean Casserole

SERVES 4

8 Italian sausages

1 tbsp olive oil

1 large onion, chopped

2 garlic cloves, chopped

1 green pepper

225g/8 oz fresh tomatoes, skinned and chopped or 400 g/14 oz can tomatoes, chopped

2 tbsp sun-dried tomato paste

400 g/14 oz can cannellini beans

mashed potato or rice, to serve

1. Using a sharp knife, deseed the pepper and cut it into thin strips.
2. Prick the Italian sausages all over with a fork. Cook the sausages, under a preheated grill, for 10–12 minutes, turning occasionally, until brown all over. Set aside and keep warm.
3. Heat the oil in a large frying pan. Add the onion, garlic and pepper to the frying pan and cook for 5 minutes, stirring occasionally, or until softened.
4. Add the tomatoes to the frying pan and leave the mixture to simmer for about 5 minutes, stirring occasionally, or until slightly reduced and thickened.
5. Stir the sun-dried tomato paste, cannellini beans and Italian sausages into the mixture in the frying pan. Cook for 4–5 minutes or until the mixture is piping hot. Add 4–5 tablespoons of water, if the mixture becomes too dry during cooking.
6. Transfer the Italian sausage and bean casserole to serving plates and serve with mashed potato or cooked rice.

Chilli Con Carne

SERVES 4

2 tbsp sunflower oil

500 g/1 lb 2 oz fresh beef mince

1 large onion, chopped

1 garlic clove, finely chopped

1 green pepper, deseeded and diced

1 tsp chilli powder

800 g/1 lb 12 oz canned chopped tomatoes

800 g/1 lb 12 oz canned red kidney beans, drained and rinsed

450 ml/16 fl oz beef stock

salt

handful of fresh coriander sprigs

2 tbsp soured cream, to serve

1. Heat the oil in a large, heavy-based saucepan or flameproof casserole. Add the beef. Cook over a medium heat, stirring frequently, for 5 minutes, or until broken up and browned.

2. Reduce the heat, add the onion, garlic and pepper and cook, stirring frequently, for 10 minutes.

3. Stir in the chilli powder, tomatoes and their juices and kidney beans. Pour in the stock and season with salt. Bring to the boil, reduce the heat and simmer, stirring frequently, for 15–20 minutes, or until the meat is tender.

4. Chop the coriander sprigs, reserving a few for a garnish, and stir into the chilli. Adjust the seasoning, if necessary. Either serve immediately with a splash of soured cream, and coriander sprigs to garnish, or leave to cool, then store in the refrigerator overnight. Reheating it the next day makes it more flavoursome.

Roast Lamb with Garlic & Rosemary

Roast Lamb with Garlic & Rosemary

SERVES 6

1 leg of lamb,

weighing 1.5 kg/3 lb 5 oz

6 garlic cloves, thinly sliced lengthways

8 fresh rosemary sprigs

salt and pepper

4 tbsp olive oil

FOR THE GLAZE

4 tbsp redcurrant jelly

300 ml/10 fl oz rosé wine

1 Preheat the oven to 200°C/400°F/Gas Mark 6. Using a small knife, cut slits all over the leg of lamb. Insert 1–2 garlic slices and 4–5 rosemary needles in each slit. Place any remaining rosemary in the base of a roasting tin. Season the lamb to taste with salt and pepper and place in the roasting tin. Pour over the oil. Cover with foil and roast for 1 hour 20 minutes.

2 Mix the redcurrant jelly and wine together in a small saucepan. Heat gently, stirring constantly, until combined. Bring to the boil, then reduce the heat and simmer until reduced. Remove the lamb from the oven and pour over the glaze. Return to the oven and cook uncovered for about 10 minutes, depending on how well done you like it.

3 Remove the lamb from the roasting tin, tent with foil and leave to rest for 15 minutes before carving and serving.

Roast Chicken

SERVES 6

1 free-range chicken, weighing 2.25 kg/5 lb

55 g/2 oz butter

2 tbsp chopped fresh lemon thyme

1 lemon, quartered

125 ml/4 fl oz white wine

salt and pepper

6 fresh thyme sprigs, to garnish

1 Preheat the oven to 220°C/425°F/Gas Mark 7. Make sure the chicken is clean, wiping it inside and out using kitchen paper, and place in a roasting tin.

2 Place the butter in a bowl and soften with a fork, then mix in the thyme and season well with salt and pepper. Butter the chicken all over with the herb butter, inside and out, and place the lemon quarters inside the body cavity. Pour the wine over the chicken.

3 Roast the chicken in the centre of the oven for 20 minutes. Reduce the temperature to 190°C/375°F/Gas Mark 5 and continue to roast for a further 1¼ hours, basting frequently. Cover with foil if the skin begins to brown too much. If the tin dries out, add a little more wine or water.

4 Test that the chicken is cooked by piercing the thickest part of the leg with a sharp knife or skewer and making sure the juices run clear. Remove from the oven.

5 Remove the chicken from the roasting tin and place on a warmed serving plate to rest, covered with foil, for 10 minutes before carving.

6 Place the roasting tin on the top of the hob and bubble the pan juices gently over a low heat until they have reduced and are thick and glossy. Season to taste with salt and pepper.

7 Serve the chicken with the pan juices and scatter with the thyme sprigs.

Quick Fixes

Quick Fixes

For those emergency times when nothing else will do! Shut out the rest of the world and lose yourself in your favourite comfort food. From cupboard to table in under an hour, try Cauliflower Cheese, or for a sweet treat choose Doughnut Muffins and a steaming mug of Hot Chocolate.

Eggs Benedict with Quick Hollandaise Sauce

Eggs Benedict with Quick Hollandaise Sauce

SERVES 4

1 tbsp white wine vinegar

4 eggs

4 English muffins

4 slices good quality ham

QUICK HOLLANDAISE SAUCE

3 egg yolks

200 g/7 oz butter

1 tbsp lemon juice

pepper

1. Fill a wide frying pan three-quarters full with water and bring to the boil over a low heat. Reduce the heat to a simmer and add the vinegar. When the water is barely shimmering, carefully break the eggs into the pan. Leave for 1 minute, then, using a large spoon, gently loosen the eggs from the bottom of the pan. Leave to cook for a further 3 minutes, or until the white is cooked and the yolk is still soft, basting the top of the egg with the water from time to time.

2. Meanwhile, to make the hollandaise sauce, place the egg yolks in a blender or food processor. Melt the butter in a small saucepan until bubbling. With the motor running, gradually add the hot butter in a steady stream until the sauce is thick and creamy. Add the lemon juice, and a little warm water if the sauce is too thick, then season to taste with pepper. Remove from the blender or food processor and keep warm.

3. Split the muffins and toast them on both sides. To serve, top each muffin with a slice of ham, a poached egg and a generous spoonful of hollandaise sauce.

Mushrooms with Rosemary, Chilli, Soured Cream & Rocket

Mushrooms with Rosemary, Chilli, Soured Cream & Rocket

SERVES 2

300 g/10½ oz button mushrooms
15 g/½ oz butter
1 tbsp vegetable oil
salt and pepper
1 small red chilli, deseeded and finely chopped
1 tbsp sour cream
2 tbsp chopped fresh parsley
1 tbsp chopped fresh rosemary
slices ciabatta bread, toasted
extra-virgin olive oil
handful of rocket leaves, to serve

1. Wipe the mushrooms with a damp cloth and slice thinly.

2. Heat the butter and vegetable oil in a wide sauté pan and add the mushrooms, stirring until well coated. Season lightly with salt and pepper and add the chopped chilli. Cover and cook for 1–2 minutes, or until the mushrooms have softened, then stir in the sour cream. Sprinkle over the chopped parsley and rosemary.

3. Serve with slices of toasted ciabatta, drizzled lightly with olive oil, topped with a few rocket leaves.

Perfect Roast Potatoes

Perfect Roast Potatoes

SERVES 6

1.3 kg/3 lb large floury potatoes, such as King Edwards, Maris Piper or Desirée, peeled and cut into even-sized chunks

salt

3 tbsp dripping, goose fat, duck fat or olive oil

1. Preheat the oven to 220ºC/425ºF/Gas Mark 7.
2. Cook the potatoes in a large saucepan of boiling salted water over a medium heat, covered, for 5–7 minutes. They will still be firm. Remove from the heat.
3. Meanwhile, add the fat to a roasting tin and place in the hot oven.
4. Drain the potatoes well and return them to the saucepan. Cover with the lid and firmly shake the pan so that the surface of the potatoes is roughened to help give a much crisper texture.
5. Remove the roasting tin from the oven and carefully tip the potatoes into the hot oil. Baste them to ensure they are all coated with the oil.
6. Roast at the top of the oven for 45–50 minutes until they are browned all over and thoroughly crisp. Turn the potatoes and baste again only once during the process or the crunchy edges will be destroyed.
7. Carefully transfer the potatoes from the roasting tin into a hot serving dish. Sprinkle with a little salt and serve at once. Any leftovers (although this is most unlikely) are delicious cold.

Chicken Tikka Masala

SERVES 4 – 6

400 g/14 oz canned chopped tomatoes

300 ml/10 fl oz double cream

8 pieces cooked tandoori chicken

fresh coriander sprigs, to garnish

FOR THE TIKKA MASALA

30 g/1 oz Ghee or 2 tbsp vegetable or groundnut oil

1 large garlic clove, finely chopped

1 fresh red chilli, deseeded and chopped

2 tsp ground cumin

2 tsp ground paprika

½ tsp salt

black pepper

1. To make the tikka masala, melt the ghee or heat the oil in a large frying pan with a lid over a medium heat. Add the garlic and chilli and stir-fry for 1 minute. Stir in the cumin, paprika, salt and pepper to taste and continue stirring for about 30 seconds.

2. Stir the tomatoes with their juices and the cream into the pan. Reduce the heat to low and leave the sauce to simmer for about 10 minutes, stirring frequently, until it reduces and thickens.

3. Meanwhile, remove all the bones and any skin from the tandoori chicken pieces, then cut the meat into bite-size pieces.

4. Adjust the seasoning of the sauce, if necessary. Add the chicken pieces to the pan, cover and leave to simmer for 3–5 minutes until the chicken is heated through. Sprinkle with the coriander to serve.

Cauliflower Cheese

SERVES 4

1 cauliflower, trimmed and cut into florets

(675 g/1 lb 8 oz prepared weight)

40 g/1½ oz butter

40 g/1½ oz plain flour

450 ml/16 fl oz milk

115 g/4 oz Cheddar cheese, finely grated

whole nutmeg

1 tbsp freshly grated Parmesan cheese

salt and pepper

1 small tomato

green salad and

crusty bread, to serve

1. Cook the cauliflower in a saucepan of lightly salted boiling water for 4–5 minutes. It should still be firm. Drain, place in a hot 1.4-litre/2½-pint gratin dish and keep warm.
2. Melt the butter in the rinsed-out saucepan over a medium heat and stir in the flour. Cook for 1 minute, stirring constantly.
3. Remove from the heat and stir in the milk gradually until you have a smooth consistency.
4. Return to a low heat and continue to stir while the sauce comes to the boil and thickens. Reduce the heat and simmer gently, stirring constantly, for about 3 minutes, or until the sauce is creamy and smooth.
5. Remove the saucepan from the heat and stir in the Cheddar cheese and a good grating of the nutmeg. Season to taste with salt and pepper.
6. Preheat the grill. Pour the hot sauce over the cauliflower, top it with the Parmesan and place under the hot grill to brown. Serve immediately with a tomato, green salad and some crusty bread.

Croque Monsieur

SERVES 2

100 g/3½ oz Gruyère or Emmenthal cheese, grated

4 slices white bread, with the crusts trimmed

2 thick slices ham

1 small egg, beaten

40 g/1½ oz unsalted butter, for frying

FOR THE WHITE SAUCE

30 g/1 oz unsalted butter

1 tsp sunflower oil

½ tbsp plain flour

125 ml/4 fl oz warm milk

pepper

1. Spread half the grated cheese on 2 slices of bread, then top each with a slice of ham, cut to fit. Sprinkle the ham with all but 2 tablespoons of the remaining cheese, then add the top slices of bread and press down.

2. To make the white sauce, melt the butter with the oil in small heavy-based saucepan over a medium heat. Stir in the flour and stir around for 1 minute to cook out the raw taste. Take the pan off the heat and pour in the milk, stirring constantly. Return the pan to the heat and continue stirring for a minute or so until the sauce is smooth and thickened. Remove the pan from the heat and stir in the remaining cheese and pepper to taste, then set aside and keep warm.

3. Beat the egg in a soup plate or other flat bowl. Add 1 sandwich and press down to coat on both sides, then remove from the bowl and repeat with the other sandwich.

4. Preheat the grill to high. Line a baking tray with foil and set aside. Melt the butter for frying in a sauté or frying pan over a medium-high heat and fry 1 or both sandwiches, depending on the size of your pan, until golden brown on both sides. Add a little extra butter, if necessary, if you have to fry the sandwiches separately.

5. Transfer the sandwiches to the foil-lined baking tray and spread the white sauce over the top. Place under the grill, about 10 cm/4 inches from the heat, and grill for 4 minutes until golden and brown.

Chive Scrambled Eggs with Brioche

Chive Scrambled Eggs with Brioche

SERVES 2

4 eggs

100 ml/3½ fl oz single cream

salt and pepper

2 tbsp snipped fresh chives, plus

4 whole fresh chives to garnish

25 g/1 oz butter

4 slices brioche loaf, lightly toasted

1. Break the eggs into a medium bowl and whisk gently with the cream. Season to taste with salt and pepper and add the snipped chives.

2. Melt the butter in a sauté pan and pour in the egg mixture. Leave to set slightly, then move the mixture towards the centre of the pan using a wooden spoon as the eggs begin to cook. Continue in this way until the eggs are cooked but still creamy.

3. Place the toasted brioche slices in the centre of 2 plates and spoon over the scrambled eggs. Serve immediately, garnished with whole chives.

Pepper Steak

SERVES 4

2 tbsp black or mixed dried peppercorns, coarsely crushed

4 fillets steaks, about 2.5 cm/1 inch thick, at room temperature

15 g/½ oz butter

1 tsp sunflower oil

4 tbsp brandy

4 tbsp crème fraîche or double optional

salt and pepper

watercress leaves, to garnish

fries, to serve

1. Spread out the crushed peppercorns on a plate and press the steaks into them to coat on both sides.

2. Melt the butter with the oil in a large sauté or frying pan over a medium-high heat. Add the steaks in a single layer and cook for 3 minutes on each side for rare; 3½ minutes on each side for medium-rare; 4 minutes on each side for medium; and 4½–5 minutes on each side for well done.

3. Transfer the steaks to a warmed plate and set aside, covering with foil to keep warm. Pour the brandy into the pan to deglaze, increase the heat and use a wooden spoon to scrape any sediment from the base of the pan. Continue boiling until reduced to around 2 tablespoons.

4. Stir in any accumulated juices from the steaks. Spoon in the crème fraîche, if using, and continue boiling until the sauce is reduced by half again. Taste, and adjust the seasoning if necessary. Spoon the pan sauce over the steaks, garnish with the watercress and serve at once with fries.

Nachos

SERVES 6

175 g/6 oz tortilla chips

400 g/14 oz canned refried beans, warmed

2 tbsp finely chopped bottled jalapeño chillies

200 g/7 oz canned or bottled pimentos or roasted peppers, drained and finely sliced

salt and pepper

115 g/4 oz Gruyère cheese, grated

115 g/4 oz Cheddar cheese, grated

guacamole and soured cream, to serve

1 Preheat the oven to 200°C/400°F/Gas Mark 6.

2 Spread the tortilla chips out over the base of a large, shallow, ovenproof dish or roasting tin. Cover with the warmed refried beans. Scatter over the chillies and pimentos and season to taste with salt and pepper. Mix the cheeses together in a bowl and sprinkle on top.

3 Bake in the preheated oven for 5–8 minutes, or until the cheese is bubbling and melted. Serve immediately with guacamole and soured cream.

Spaghetti alla Carbonara

SERVES 4

450 g/1 lb dried spaghetti

175 g/6 oz rindless streaky bacon, diced

1 garlic clove, finely chopped

3 eggs, lightly beaten

salt and pepper

4 tbsp fresh Parmesan cheese shavings

1. Bring a large, heavy-based saucepan of lightly salted water to the boil. Add the pasta, return to the boil and cook for 8–10 minutes, or until tender but still firm to the bite.

2. Meanwhile, cook the bacon and garlic in a heavy-based, dry frying pan over a medium heat for 5 minutes, or until crisp-tender. Remove from the frying pan and drain on kitchen paper.

3. Drain the pasta and return it to the saucepan, but do not return to the heat. Add the bacon and garlic and the eggs. Season to taste with salt and pepper. Toss thoroughly with 2 large forks. Add half the Parmesan cheese and toss again. Transfer to a warmed serving dish, sprinkle with the remaining Parmesan cheese and serve immediately.

Risotto with Four Cheeses

Risotto with Four Cheeses

SERVES 6

1 litre/1¾ pints vegetable stock

40 g/1½ oz unsalted butter

1 onion, chopped finely

350 g/12 oz arborio rice

200 ml/7 fl oz dry white wine

55 g/2 oz Gorgonzola cheese, crumbled

55 g/2 oz freshly grated taleggio cheese

55 g/2 oz freshly grated fontina cheese

55 g/2 oz freshly grated Parmesan cheese

salt and pepper

2 tbsp chopped fresh flat-leaf parsley, to garnish

1. Pour the stock into a large saucepan and bring to the boil. Lower the heat and simmer gently.

2. Melt the butter in another large, heavy-based saucepan. Add the onion and cook over a low heat, stirring occasionally, for 5 minutes, until softened. Add the rice and cook, stirring constantly, for 2–3 minutes, until all the grains are thoroughly coated and glistening.

3. Add the wine and cook, stirring constantly, until it has almost completely evaporated. Add a ladleful of the hot stock and cook, stirring constantly, until all the stock has been absorbed. Continue cooking, stirring and adding the stock, a ladleful at a time, for about 20 minutes, or until the rice is tender and the liquid has been absorbed.

4. Remove the saucepan from the heat and stir in the Gorgonzola, taleggio, fontina and about one quarter of the Parmesan until melted. Season to taste with salt and pepper. Transfer the risotto to a warmed serving dish, sprinkle with the remaining Parmesan, garnish with the parsley and serve immediately.

Fusilli with Gorgonzola and Mushroom Sauce

SERVES 4

350 g/12 oz dried spaghetti

3 tbsp olive oil

350 g/12 oz wild mushrooms, sliced

1 garlic clove, chopped finely

400 ml/14 fl oz double cream

250 g/9 oz Gorgonzola cheese, crumbled

salt and pepper

2 tbsp chopped fresh flat-leaf parsley, to garnish

1. Bring a large saucepan of lightly salted water to the boil. Add the pasta, bring back to the boil and cook for 8–10 minutes, until tender, but still firm to the bite.

2. Meanwhile, heat the olive oil in a heavy-based saucepan. Add the mushrooms and cook over a low heat, stirring frequently, for 5 minutes. Add the garlic and cook for a further 2 minutes.

3. Add the cream, bring to the boil and cook for 1 minute, until slightly thickened. Stir in the cheese and cook over a low heat until it has melted. Do not allow the sauce to boil, once the cheese has been added. Season to taste with salt and pepper and remove the saucepan from the heat.

4. Drain the pasta and tip it into the sauce. Toss well to coat, then serve immediately, garnished with the parsley.

Chunky Vegetable Soup

Chunky Vegetable Soup

SERVES 6

2 carrots, sliced

1 onion, diced

1 garlic clove, crushed

350 g/12 oz new potatoes, diced

2 celery sticks, sliced

115 g/4 oz closed-cup mushrooms, quartered

400 g/14 oz canned chopped tomatoes in tomato juice

600 ml/1 pint vegetable stock

1 bay leaf

1 tsp dried mixed herbs or 1 tbsp chopped fresh mixed herbs

85 g/3 oz sweetcorn kernels, frozen or canned, drained

55 g/2 oz green cabbage, shredded

freshly ground black pepper

few sprigs of fresh basil, to garnish

crusty wholemeal or white bread rolls, to serve

1. Put the carrots, onion, garlic, potatoes, celery, mushrooms, tomatoes and stock into a large saucepan. Stir in the bay leaf and herbs. Bring to the boil, then reduce the heat, cover and simmer for 25 minutes.

2. Add the sweetcorn and cabbage and return to the boil. Reduce the heat, cover and simmer for 5 minutes, or until the vegetables are tender. Remove and discard the bay leaf. Season to taste with pepper.

3. Ladle into warmed bowls and garnish with basil. Serve immediately with crusty bread rolls.

Apple Pancakes with Maple Syrup Butter

Apple Pancakes with Maple Syrup Butter

SERVES 4 – 6

200 g/7 oz self-raising flour

100 g/3½ oz caster sugar

1 tsp ground cinnamon

1 egg

200 ml/7 fl oz milk

2 apples, peeled and grated

1 tsp butter

MAPLE SYRUP BUTTER

85 g/3 oz butter, softened

3 tbsp maple syrup

1. Mix the flour, sugar and cinnamon together in a bowl and make a well in the centre. Beat the egg and the milk together and pour into the well. Using a wooden spoon, gently incorporate the dry ingredients into the liquid until well combined, then stir in the grated apple.

2. Heat the butter in a large non-stick frying pan over a low heat until melted and bubbling. Add tablespoons of the pancake mixture to form 9-cm/3½-inch circles. Cook each pancake for about 1 minute, until it starts to bubble lightly on the top and looks set, then flip it over and cook the other side for 30 seconds, or until cooked through. The pancakes should be golden brown; if not, increase the heat a little. Remove from the pan and keep warm. Repeat the process until all of the pancake batter has been used up (it is not necessary to add extra butter).

3. To make the maple syrup butter, melt the butter with the maple syrup in a saucepan over a low heat and stir until combined. To serve, place the pancakes on serving dishes and spoon over the flavoured butter. Serve warm.

SERVES 4 – 6

100 g/3 1/2 oz plain chocolate, with at least 70% cocoa, broken up

600 ml/1 pint milk

115 g/4 oz caster sugar

3 1/2 tbsp cornflour

1 tsp vanilla essence

pinch salt

Hot Chocolate

1. Melt the chocolate in the milk in a heavy-based saucepan over a medium heat, stirring constantly. Add the sugar and continue stirring until it dissolves.

2. Put the cornflour in a small bowl and make a well in the centre. Add about 2 tablespoons of the hot liquid and gradually stir the cornflour into the liquid until a thick, smooth paste forms. Stir in another 2 tablespoons of hot liquid.

3. Stir all the cornflour mixture into the saucepan and bring to a simmer, stirring. Bring to the boil and continue stirring until the chocolate thickens. Pour into coffee cups and serve.

Strawberries & Cream Milk Shake

SERVES 2

150 g/5 1/2 oz frozen strawberries

100 ml/3 1/2 fl oz single cream

200 ml/7 fl oz cold full-cream milk

1 tbsp caster sugar

mint leaves, to decorate

1 Put the strawberries, cream, milk and caster sugar into a food processor and process until smooth.

2 Pour into glasses and serve decorated with mint leaves.

Buttermilk Scones

MAKES 8

55 g/2 oz cold butter, cut into pieces, plus extra for greasing

300 g/10½ oz self-raising flour, plus extra for dusting

1 tsp baking powder

pinch of salt

40 g/1½ oz golden caster sugar

300 ml/10 fl oz buttermilk

2 tbsp milk

whipped cream and strawberry jam, to serve

1. Preheat the oven to 220°C/425°F/Gas Mark 7, then grease a baking sheet. Sift the flour, baking powder and salt into a bowl. Add the butter and rub in until the mixture resembles fine breadcrumbs. Add the sugar and buttermilk and quickly mix together.

2. Turn the mixture out on to a floured work surface and knead lightly. Roll out to 2.5 cm/1 inch thick. Using a 6-cm/2½-inch plain or fluted cutter, stamp out scones and place on the prepared baking sheet. Gather the trimmings, re-roll and stamp out more scones until all the dough is used up.

3. Brush the tops of the scones with milk. Bake in the preheated oven for 12–15 minutes, or until well risen and golden. Transfer to a wire rack to cool. Split and serve with whipped cream and strawberry jam.

Doughnut Muffins

MAKES 12

175 g/6 oz butter, softened, plus extra for greasing

200 g/7 oz caster sugar

2 large eggs, lightly beaten

375 g/13 oz plain flour

¾ tbsp baking powder

¼ tsp bicarbonate of soda

pinch of salt

½ tsp freshly grated nutmeg

250 ml/9 fl oz milk

TOPPING

100 g/3½ oz caster sugar

1 tsp ground cinnamon

25 g/1 oz butter, melted

1. Preheat the oven to 180°C/350°F/Gas Mark 4. Grease a deep 12-cup muffin tin.

2. In a large bowl, beat the butter and sugar together until light and creamy. Add the eggs, a little at a time, beating well between additions.

3. Sift the flour, baking powder, bicarbonate of soda, salt and nutmeg together. Add half to the creamed mixture with half of the milk. Gently fold the ingredients together before incorporating the remaining flour and milk. Spoon the mixture into the prepared muffin tin, filling each hole to about two-thirds full. Bake for 15-20 minutes, or until the muffins are lightly brown and firm to the touch.

4. For the topping, mix the sugar and cinnamon together. While the muffins are still warm from the oven, brush lightly with melted butter and sprinkle over the cinnamon and sugar mixture. Eat warm or cold.

Waffles with Caramelized Bananas

MAKES 12

175 g/6 oz plain flour

2 tsp baking powder

½ tsp salt

2 tsp caster sugar

2 eggs, separated

250 ml/9 fl oz milk

85 g/3 oz butter, melted

CARAMELIZED BANANAS

100 g/3½ oz butter, cut into pieces

3 tbsp golden syrup

3 large ripe bananas, peeled and thickly sliced

1. Mix the flour, baking powder, salt and sugar together in a bowl. Whisk the egg yolks, milk and melted butter together with a fork, then stir this mixture into the dry ingredients to make a smooth batter.

2. Using an electric mixer or hand whisk, whisk the egg whites in a clean glass bowl until stiff peaks form. Fold into the batter mixture. Spoon 2 large tablespoons of the batter into a preheated waffle maker and cook according to the manufacturer's instructions.

3. To make the caramelized bananas, melt the butter with the golden syrup in a saucepan over a low heat and stir until combined. Leave to simmer for a few minutes until the caramel thickens and darkens slightly. Add the bananas and mix gently to coat. Pour over the warm waffles and serve immediately.

Nutty Chocolate Drizzles

MAKES 24

225 g/8 oz butter or margarine, plus extra for greasing
275 g/9½ oz demerara sugar
1 egg
140g/5 oz plain flour, sifted
1 tsp baking powder
1 tsp bicarbonate of soda
125 g/4½ oz rolled oats
20 g/¾ oz bran
20 g/¾ oz wheatgerm
115 g/4 oz mixed nuts, toasted and chopped roughly
90 g/3¼ oz plain chocolate chips
115 g/4 oz raisins and sultanas
175 g/6 oz plain chocolate, chopped roughly

1 Preheat the oven to 180°C/350°F/Gas Mark 4. Grease a large baking sheet. In a large bowl, cream together the butter, sugar and egg. Add the flour, baking powder, bicarbonate of soda, oats, bran and wheatgerm and mix together until well combined. Stir in the nuts, chocoate chips and dried fruit.

2 Put 24 rounded tablespoonfuls of the cookie mixture onto the greased baking sheet. Transfer to the preheated oven and bake for 12 minutes, or until the cookies are golden brown.

3 Remove the cookies from the oven, transfer to a wire rack and let them cool. While they are cooling, put the chocolate pieces into a heatproof bowl over a pan of gently simmering water and heat until melted. Stir the chocolate, then allow to cool slightly. Use a spoon to drizzle the chocolate in waves over the cookies, or spoon it into a piping nozzle and pipe zigzag lines over the cookies. Store in an airtight container in the refrigerator before serving.

Chewy Golden Cookies

MAKES 30

175 g/6 oz butter or margarine, plus extra for greasing

275 g/9½ oz light muscovado sugar

225 ml/8 fl oz golden syrup

3 egg whites

500 g/1 lb 2 oz rolled oats

280 g/10 oz plain flour

pinch of salt

1 tsp baking powder

icing sugar, to drizzle

1. Preheat the oven to 180°C/350°F/Gas Mark 4 and grease a large baking sheet.
2. In a large mixing bowl, blend the butter (or margarine, if using), sugar, syrup and egg whites together. Gradually add the oats, flour, salt and baking powder and mix thoroughly.
3. Drop 30 rounded tablespoonfuls of the mixture onto the baking sheet and transfer to the preheated oven.
4. Bake for 12 minutes, or until the cookies are light brown.
5. Remove from the oven and let them cool on a wire rack. Drizzle over the icing sugar and serve.

index

A
apples
  apple pancakes with maple syrup butter 115
  apple and plum crumble 8

B
bacon and ham
  croque monsieur 100
  eggs benedict with quick hollandaise sauce 92
  spaghetti alla carbonara 107
bananas
  carrot cake 43
  waffles with caramelized bananas 122
beans
  chilli con carne 85
  nachos 106
  sausage and bean casserole 84
beef
  baked lasagne 73
  chilli con carne 85
  Italian steak melt burgers 58
  pepper steak 104
  spaghetti with meatballs 60
  tagliatelle with rich meat sauce 65
  winter beef stew with herb dumplings 78
blueberries
  blueberry and lemon drizzle cake 37
  Manhattan cheesecake 25

C
carrot cake 43
cauliflower cheese 99
cheese
  cauliflower cheese 99
  cheese gratin 77
  cheese and tomato pizza 54
  croque monsieur 100
  deep chocolate cheesecake 46
  fusilli with Gorgonzola and mushroom sauce 111
  Italian steak melt burgers 58
  Manhattan cheesecake 25
  nachos 106
  risotto with four cheeses 108
Chelsea buns 13
cherries
  chocolate and cherry tiramisù 47
  latticed cherry pie 21
chicken
  chicken fajitas 82
  chicken tikka masala 98
  coq au vin 70
  roast chicken 89
chocolate
  caramel chocolate shortbread 33
  chocolate and cherry tiramisù 47
  chocolate chip ice cream with hot chocolate fudge sauce 40
  chocolate chip muffins 17
  chocolate fudge cake 34
  chocolate mousse 39
  deep chocolate cheesecake 46
  double chocolate brownies 29
  fine chocolate tart 18
  hot chocolate 116
  Mississippi mud cake 22
  nutty chocolate drizzles 125
  profiteroles 12
courgettes
  courgette pie 68
  roasted vegetable moussaka 69
crème caramel 28
custard 38

E
eggs
  chive scrambled eggs with brioche 103
  eggs benedict with quick hollandaise sauce 92
  spaghetti alla carbonara 107

F
fisherman's pie 62

I
ice cream
  chocolate chip ice cream with hot chocolate fudge sauce 40
  raspberry ripple 14
  rich vanilla 11

J
jam roly-poly 38

L
lamb
  roast lamb with garlic and rosemary 86
  shepherd's pie 74
leeks: creamy leek bake 57
lemons
  blueberry and lemon drizzle cake 37
  lemon meringue pie 30

M
muffins
  chocolate chip muffins 17
  doughnut muffins 121
  English muffins 26
mushrooms
  fusilli with Gorgonzola and mushroom sauce 111
  mushrooms with rosemary, chilli, soured cream and rocket 95
  oven-baked risotto with mushrooms 61

N
nuts
  carrot cake 43
  creamy leek bake 57
  nutty chocolate drizzles 125

O
oats
  chewy golden cookies 126
  nutty chocolate drizzles 125

P
pasta
  baked lasagne 73
  fusilli with Gorgonzola and mushroom sauce 111
  spaghetti alla carbonara 107
  spaghetti with meatballs 60
  tagliatelle with rich meat sauce 65
pizza, cheese and tomato 54
pork
  baked lasagne 73
  spare ribs 66
potatoes
  baked potatoes with pesto 81
  cheese gratin 77
  fisherman's pie 62
  perfect roast potatoes 96
  sausages and mash with onion gravy 53
  shepherd's pie 74

R
raspberries
  raspberry ripple ice cream 14
  trifle 44
rice
  courgette pie 68
  oven-baked risotto with mushrooms 61
  risotto with four cheeses 108

S
sausages
  sausage and bean casserole 84
  sausages and mash with onion gravy 53
scones, buttermilk 118
strawberries and cream milk shake 117

T
tomatoes
  cheese and tomato pizza 54
  roasted tomato soup 50
trifle 44

V
vegetable soup, chunky 112

W
waffles with caramelized bananas 122